THE FRONTIERS OF DRAMA

THE FRONTIERS OF DRAMA

by

UNA ELLIS-FERMOR

NEW YORK

OXFORD UNIVERSITY PRESS

1946

IN MEMORIAM

PRINTED IN GREAT BRITAIN

PREFACE

THIS book is an attempt to investigate some of the means by which an art form (in this case, drama) may transcend its normal and seemingly inevitable limitations. It is therefore the picture of a conflict, now between form and some stubborn content that resists inclusion, now between the dramatic process and the limitations of a medium that is nevertheless essential. It thus resolves itself into a series of studies of specific and characteristic areas of conflict, of those frontiers on which the limitations are met; a study, that is, of certain plays which achieve ' of all things not impossible the most difficult ' and transcend their apparently immutable boundaries; a study simultaneously of certain traditions, skills, devices, or inventions through which the disadvantages inherent in the form are circumvented or turned to account. The frontiers of drama, it would seem, expand and contract from age to age, and the nature of the expansion can best be seen in those rare plays which by a supreme reach of art contrive to break through or transcend what seem their natural limits.

To explore this field systematically would need a quite different kind of book, more general and abstract in treatment and more formidable in extent. The present essays can be regarded only as preliminary to such a study; they contain some of the reflections which have occurred to me in the course of twenty years' consideration of the practice of many dramatists of widely differing kinds, of the theories implicit in their practice, and of certain underlying aesthetic laws to which the accumulated theory and practice of more than two thousand years would appear to point. I have drawn my conclusions from the drama of Europe or of European derivation, for the problems raised by the various forms of Asiatic drama and, still more, primitive drama would involve extension and qualification for which there is at the present date no room. No comprehensive survey of the

v

underlying laws which determine the limitations of drama could safely be attempted without consideration of all surviving or credibly reported kinds, nor would such consideration necessarily save the conclusions from the danger of all *a posteriori* deductions. For this reason, among others, I have cast this preliminary study in the form of a few simple studies of individual plays or of specific aspects of dramatic technique.

U. E.-F.

January 1945

ACKNOWLEDGEMENTS

I WISH to acknowledge the courteous permission of Mr. T. S. Eliot to quote a passage from *The Family Reunion*, of Mr. Louis MacNeice to quote from his translation of the *Agamemnon* and of Messrs. Faber and Faber for the like permission on their part.

My thanks are due to various friends who have helped me either with specific reference or with discussions of the ideas in this book: to my father for general assistance in the preparation for the press and for much else; to Dr. Marianne Pick and Professor Dorothy Tarrant for checking specific details in the respective fields of German and of Greek drama, though for any errors in these fields I alone am responsible; to Sofie Mess and Dr. George Brightman for discussion of the work of Ibsen and of the underlying fallacy in the chapter on Tragedy respectively; to Grace Corson O'Conor, in whose home the greater part of this book was written or revised.

My debt to the thought and knowledge of previous scholars and critics, living or dead, American, Continental, and English, is too great either to be acknowledged in detail or to be passed over in silence.

PREFACE TO SECOND EDITION

NO alterations have been made in this edition, though six typographical errors which escaped my notice in the proofs of the first have been kindly noted by friends and duly corrected.

I should like to take this opportunity of acknowledging the many constructive criticisms that I have received from correspondents (not least from those who differed from my conclusions) and to express my gratitude for the suggestions thus generously communicated.

U. E.-F.

May 1946

CONTENTS

CHAPTER ONE

THE LIMITATIONS OF DRAMA

THE limitations of drama are frontiers that are difficult to define precisely, though we all know approximately where they lie. They relate it to and distinguish it from the literary forms that lie nearest to it, and they are imposed not by the surrounding forms but from within. For an art has this in common with an organism, that its embryo carries within itself certain principles that determine its growth and features. Its limitations are thus an aspect of its quality, and though this quality may be modified by conditions or by artificial restrictions, this can happen only to a slight degree; conditions far beyond anything we can readily imagine would be needed to induce the seed of a Lombardy poplar to produce the form and habit of a cactus. There is always something irreducible which is inherent and peculiar to the organism.

In an art such as drama we can see this ineradicable, inherent individuality at work whenever we watch it taking shape. We could begin, for instance, by looking at the group of related characteristics that are shared by all great plays, no matter how widely they vary, and from them we might abstract a type, a form that could never be confused with any other. This is to begin at the final product and draw our inferences from the results of the process; a natural way to go about the business, once we have observed, as few of us can avoid doing to-day, that there *is* an art of drama and that it is markedly different from fiction, verse narrative, lyric, epic, or any other form. It is easier to say what lies well within the compass of drama than to say what lies upon its borders, and we may perhaps pause to remind ourselves first of that.

Strong passions at work in the theatre of the world are so far characteristic of the material on which the major dramatists have always drawn as to seem essential to great drama; love, hate, ambition, jealousy lie clearly within the area of human experience from which it draws most fruitfully. Without the tension and balance that result from the conflict of these passions with the world they seek to subdue to their purposes, we cannot imagine such drama. Again, a brief, shapely series of related deeds, such as sometimes emerges from the chaos of event in daily life or historical record, is as closely akin to the form of drama as strong conflicting passion is to its mood, and here again we recognize something essential to drama; material whose scope and shapeliness seem half-way already to dramatic form. Finally, a certain grand simplicity of idea, relating these passions and events in an interpretation that, while sensitive and undogmatic, can yet comprehend and shape them, is the kind of thought which can best be conveyed in the brief form of a play. Therefore the passions of Clytemnestra, Electra, Oedipus, Othello, Macbeth, and Brand, powerfully entangled in the world they move in, find artistic expression in drama; the life of Faust draws one dramatist after another to reproduce it; Aeschylus's belief in the suffering that brings wisdom has ordered his great trilogy to a harmony still unsurpassed. In material such as this, we should all agree, are the essentials of drama, in mood, in form, and in thought.

Another way of studying the working of this innate tendency, and one which brings us rather nearer to the question with which we are concerned, is to consider how drama uses the raw material of life upon which it, in common with all the arts, draws for its subsistence. By the selections it makes, by its adjustment of emphasis, the nature of the art as a whole will be revealed, no less surely than is that of some individual playwright when we watch his transmutation of his sources.

A third body of evidence for the existence of this irreducible principle inherent in an art is also partly available in the case of drama; the process of its evolution. Unfortunately we have here only partial evidence and there is not enough for firm generalization. But a prolonged study of the rise of Western European drama and its development from four sentences in the Mass to a form which can be related in all essentials to that of the Greek drama with which no contact had been maintained,[1] convinces me that, if we had for other bodies of drama (Greek or Asiatic) as full a record of the earliest phases as we have for Western Europe, we should find similar progressions from the non-dramatic to the dramatic, in accordance with the same innate principle. I believe that we should then be in a position to make the generalization that I am withheld from making absolutely : that the essentials of dramatic form are the inevitable expression of that dramatic sense which is an indestructible part of the human imagination; that when this dramatic sense is suffered to develop fully and reach complete expression, no matter what be the race, the age, or the starting-point, the final product will always be essentially the same. If I plant six acorns, some of them may fail to germinate, some may die, and some be stunted; but if they produce anything, they will produce oaks.

Perhaps I have said enough to suggest that I think there is an individuality inherent in any art form (and certainly in drama, with which I am here concerned) that broadly determines its nature. It is not, that is to say, the mere sport of circumstance; form, here as elsewhere, is the embodiment of an absolute principle. We may perhaps make this a little clearer by going back to the second of the two ways we suggested for observing the operation of this individuality— that of the characteristic selection made by drama from the mass of raw material upon which all art draws. Is there, that is to say, some material which is more readily shaped into drama and other material which offers a more stubborn resistance; can the limitations of drama, or some of them, be discovered by what it can and what it cannot subdue to its form?

This is a difficult question to answer as it stands, and if we demanded an absolute answer it would become an impossible one; we would hesitate to say of any given kind of material that it could never be shaped into drama, that no dramatist could have transmuted it and no future

[1] I distinguish here between continuity in drama and continuity in certain arts of the theatre. The case for the continuity of histrionic art through the transition period has been made convincingly by certain historians of the Theatre, such as Sir Edmund Chambers. (See *The Medieval Stage*, Vol. I, Books 1, 2.)

dramatist ever will. But we can qualify our answer and say that there are certain kinds of material which have been generally avoided or attempted only with manifest difficulty or disaster, and that even by dramatists of strong native ability working at a time when dramatic art was both vigorous and mature. Certain areas of human emotion and experience, certain series of events, certain regions of thought are peculiarly intractable to drama even though they are not impracticable to other forms of art, even to other forms of literature,[1] just as there are others that seem to suggest dramatic treatment as naturally as certain landscapes seem to demand treatment in oil rather than in water-colour, gouache, or pastel. To this extent, as Pirandello indicated, material may be regarded as ' in search of an author '.

But what actually happens out upon the borders? There, if we are right in believing every form to have its own limitations, imposed by its own powers, we should come upon material which is either doubtfully dramatic or undramatic in much the same way as the material we briefly considered a page or two earlier was innately dramatic. Can we go so far as to keep the divisions we then used and look for the opposite of what we then found, for material which is innately obstinate and unsusceptible to dramatic treatment, by reason, in one case, of the emotional experience from which it derives, in another of the scope and relation of its events and in a third of the nature of the idea which lies behind it? I think we can find in each case at least one type of material which resists dramatic form.

Is there, to begin with the first of these, any significant part of man's emotional experience which has consistently proved difficult or nearly impossible to subdue to dramatic form? Is there any passion the experience of which is incompatible with the essential mood of drama? There is, I think, one vast and significant area which has given rise to less great drama than any other of even comparable significance. The history of the attempt to write religious drama

---

[1] I am not here discussing, of course, the practicability of transmuting Pythagoras's theorem or the Quantum Theory into drama. Material of that kind is ruled out at an earlier stage in the classification of the matter and form of art, on the ground that it is not, so far as can be observed or foreseen, suitable matter for expression in any art-form.

is a long record of failures or partial successes, and it would
seem that religious experience is just such an area as we have
postulated. Nor is it difficult to suggest a reason for this
long record of sterility, for the failure springs directly from
the incompatibility between the raw material which affords
the content and the form which attempts to assimilate it.
It is not an accident that the main body of medieval ' religious ' drama and of much that succeeds it is not concerned
with any essential part of religious experience, but preoccupied instead either with illustrating the dogmas or
ethics incidental to some specific form of organized belief,
or with presenting some aspect of the conflict set up by the
claims of this ethic and other passions which actually form
the main tissue of the play. There are several hundred plays
of this kind, but how often do we find a play in which the
fire and illumination that is the essence of religious experience
becomes the central force, as Macbeth's ambition, Othello's
jealousy, Clytemnestra's hatred become the central force
of their plays, transmuting the characters, controlling the
events, and modifying lives and fates ? These other passions
are compatible with drama, but there seems to be a deep
antagonism between religious emotion and the needs of
dramatic art. Nor is this conclusion altogether unexpected,
for the essence of religious experience is that union, which
all mystics know in greater or less degree, according to their
capacity, of man's spirit with a spiritual reality beyond yet
akin to him. The mood, the condition of spirit, which is the
climax of this experience is beatitude, a condition free from
conflict within the mind and unconcerned by conflict without.
And in saying this we have implied the elimination of that
very conflict upon whose tension and balance the significant
form of drama depends. This material, that is to say,
refuses to drama one of the fundamental conditions of its
being, and the dramatist who attempts it is likely to find
himself crippled, not by the lack of passion in his subject,
but, paradoxically, by its dominance. Who, upon reflection, would hope to make great drama out of the life of
St. Dominic ? Yet where, outside the records of the Old
Testament prophets, could we find passion burning itself
more rapidly and irresistibly through whatever attempted to

oppose it? It is this irresistible power itself that destroys
the balanced conflict upon which tragic drama depends. It
is sometimes suggested in explanation that the magnitude
and profundity of the experience themselves carry it beyond
the bounds of artistic presentation : ' When I consider the
heavens, the work of Thy hands, what is man? . . .' But
it is not here, I think, that the real difficulty lies. What it
is possible for man to experience it is possible for the shaping
spirit of poetic imagination in part at least to reveal. We
need go no further than the immortal witness of the *Paradiso*
to realize that it is with the specific form of drama that the
material is in conflict and that the incompatibility is one of
kind, not of degree.

Can we now in the same way discover another kind of
material which, though it can be shaped readily into some
other literary form, resists that of drama, not, this time,
because its mood is incompatible with dramatic tension, but
because its scope and the natural relation of its events cannot
be reduced or extended to the length of a play? Because, that
is to say, the matter is unsuitable, in spite of its having a
natural form, in spite of the sequence of historical events or
of observed experience having a true beginning, middle, and
end? Is the distinction, for instance, between the raw
material of epic and the raw material of drama a fundamental one? Is there any æsthetic reason why, to take the
opposite case, a playwright should not create great tragic
drama out of the elements that had originally suggested a
single-scene play?

I think the second suggestion may be dismissed at once,
because such an extension of character, event, and idea must
either reduce the original scene to an episode in a larger and
more complex action or elaborate it into something quite
other than it was in the beginning. The acorn will again
refuse, with customary obstinacy, to produce anything but
an oak. But the challenge of epic material to a dramatist is
a more serious problem. On the one hand, it is obvious that
single episodes or parts of actual epics or of bodies of saga-
material may themselves be the natural material of drama.
On the other hand, there would seem at first glance nothing
against compressing what has already been treated in a more

extended form, since severe selection and condensation are
natural processes in dramatization. But neither of these
statements touches the real problem. The shape of a single
episode or fragment may be of a nature quite other than the
shape of the whole, while compression of epic matter no more
results in anything equivalent to epic than compression of
Tom Jones would result in anything equivalent to the stories
in *Life's Handicap*. It is one thing to pillage a mass of saga-
material for what is dramatic in it; it is another to present
the whole of that material, its scope and architecture, the
extent and relation of its parts, in any form but the one
which naturally does this, the epic itself. The brevity of
drama, which is inseparable from its concentration and its
immediacy, makes this inevitable. Hardy's *The Dynasts* is
rather an epic poem in dramatic form than a drama, not
because it is an intractable stage play,[1] but because the
peculiar balance and articulation of the parts—the multi-
farious episode and detail, the interplay of passion and
event with detached commentary and speculation—arising
from the very nature of the matter the poet has chosen,
destroy that concentration from which derives the significant
form of drama. Milton, that great structural artist, abandoned the scheme for a play on the subject of *Paradise Lost*,
though he explored it long and carefully. It would be a rash
man who would attempt a great tragedy on the history of
the Jewish captivity, but Hebbel moved as unerringly as
Euripides when he selected the episode of *Judith*. One of
the actual limitations of drama against which the greatest
dramatists have often chafed is its refusal to display the
multifariousness of life. Aeschylus, Shakespeare, and a few
others devise their own methods for circumventing it.

Are there, finally, any underlying ideas which are peculiarly
difficult to express in drama? For upon some interpretation
of the universe, not dogmatic, not even as a rule explicit,
but fundamental and comprehensive, all great drama in the
last resort depends. It is not easy to put that of any great

[1] On the irrelevance of this as a test of dramatic form, in general and
in the particular case of *The Dynasts*, see Lascelles Abercrombie, *Thomas
Hardy* (1912), Chapter VIII, and for Hardy's brief statement of the
same view of his own ' epic drama ', see his preface to the 1903 and
subsequent editions.

dramatist in the form of an abstract statement—if it were, he would probably be not a great dramatist, but a philosopher *manqué*—yet we apprehend it, to the measure of our capacity, and it is vitally related to the form of the play. Now, is it possible for a dramatist, while still approaching the universe of experience as a dramatist, to hold an interpretation which resists dramatic form? I am not, of course, referring to confusion in the dramatist's own mind, but to a reading of life which, however clearly and deeply he has apprehended it, is yet antagonistic to drama. I think it is possible, and I think we can say broadly that there are some plays which, while they impress us with the magnitude and power of their underlying thought, give us also the impression either that the thought is imperfectly imaged or that the attempt to image it has damaged the play. I am never entirely satisfied, for instance, that our tendency to think of Ibsen's *Emperor and Galilean* as a medley of contradictory and unreconciled ideas is not merely a misunderstanding of a play which attempts more than drama can comprehend. The second part of Goethe's *Faust*, in the same way, loses dramatic form, not, like *The Dynasts*, because it contains the stuff of epic, with its essentially different tempo and process, but because, like *Emperor and Galilean*, the underlying interpretation demands too complex a manifestation. In a lesser degree, three at least of the Jacobeans—Chapman, Webster, and Tourneur—are gripped by this dilemma, though in Chapman there is a certain amount of mere confusion as well. Looked at beside the grand, hard lines of Aeschylus's thought, these widely differing interpretations all alike reveal a multifariousness of detail similar to the multifariousness of event in epic material. This does not mean that they are vast areas of ideas only loosely connected, ill-organized as the decorations of a façade of a bad architectural period. They are all organisms consisting of related parts of which the most minute are themselves significant; systems of independent ideas in which the qualifications of the main generalization are inseparable from the life of the whole. But this vitality and coherence themselves break the mould of the plays in which they are imaged. Ibsen's *Emperor and Galilean* is not merely a series of interesting and vivid pictures of life in the fourth century, seen from a bewildering number of angles and in terms of a bewildering succession of individuals and groups; Ibsen comprehends in his own imaginative experience the chaos of conflicting thoughts, emotions, creeds, and customs, and out of this strife there emerges a vision that contains and transcends the separate and conflicting ideals. No power on earth could convey to us this vision of transcendent harmony without first laying before us, patiently and minutely, the multitudinous confusion and conflict of purposed and purposeless energy, the experience of a world in which thought and belief are made and unmade by the ceaseless fecundity of decay. But equally no power on earth, not even Ibsen's at the height of its strength, could compass this in a single play, and *Emperor and Galilean* is a failure— one of those failures that give deeper assurance of the magnitude of man's destiny than all but the noblest of his triumphs. Ibsen's interpretation, at that stage, of the nature of man's experience and destiny is so finely articulated and so complex that he cannot use the clear, firm lines in which dramatic form normally images underlying thought. In *Faust* also, where the poet's intention is even less purely dramatic, we find that incompatibility between the basic idea and the dramatic form has carried it clean out of the category of drama, and much that is most intractable escapes into passages of lyric and speculative poetry. Chapman's complex theory of the nature of statecraft and the relations of the state and the individual (which he had perhaps apprehended but imperfectly himself) led to a series of breakdowns, not only in structure but in character itself; Webster's vision of the relations between good and evil struggles, through the first four acts of both plays, with the supremacy of the plot and, in the final scenes, takes precedence of it; Tourneur's *Atheist's Tragedy* is the helpless victim of a reading of life which he can hardly transmute at all into dramatic form. We have found, that is, a few instances of the kind of interpretation which, if forced into dramatic form, tends to destroy its essential character.

Here, briefly, are three aspects of the conflict between content and form, those which first cross our minds when we ask ourselves in what ways drama is limited by its own

B

powers. And in pushing out to the borderline of drama, we have touched, it will be seen, the boundaries of other literary forms, of epic, of lyric, of narrative and reflective prose, which equally have their own borderlines and their own limitations. But the same conflict may arise not between potential content and the mood, scope, or shape essential to drama, but between content and the technical medium which drama forces it to use. There are some kinds of material which rebel against the technical limitations of direct speech; parts of what a dramatist desires and needs to convey to his audience refuse to go into the mouths of any of the characters and he is driven to adopt conventions (momentary suspensions of dramatic illusion) or to elaborate technical devices to break through or circumvent this kind of limitation. This conflict can generally be traced in certain details in the play; in the difficulties the dramatist meets in conveying some of the thoughts in the minds of his characters which would not normally be spoken aloud, or in keeping before our minds something essential to our understanding of the play which is not necessarily in the minds of any of the characters. And chorus, soliloquy, imagery, and prosody may all be means of transcending this limitation, of achieving fullness of content without losing concentration or probability.

Now, this is of some interest, for when we observe the dramatist's struggle with the limitations of his medium, now by a bold use of convention, now by means of the significant functions of imagery and prosody, we realize that the natural conflict between content and form is to certain dramatists, and these among the greatest, no deterrent, but a challenge. Is this also true in those other conflicts that we have just considered? Does intransigence of material challenge a dramatist as well as intransigence of medium, and that on a greater scale and to greater issues? Can we, if that is so, reconsider and perhaps qualify what we have said, and admit that even those regions that are most forbidding have been mastered from time to time by the dramatists great enough to reconcile the conflict? I think we can.

For in a certain sense and for some dramatists, the limitations exist to be transcended. Difficulty is opportunity, and some rare and noble pieces of art owe their quality to the taking up of this challenge. The achievement that was beyond the reach of many men lies just within the power of another; apparently irreducible material is subdued to that form with which his individual aspiration associated it. Perhaps of all dramatists Aeschylus and Shakespeare show the largest number of these strange victories snatched from apparently certain defeat. But we may find them where we least expect them, on the grand scale or in the treatment of some detail of technique. We can, moreover, upon reflection, find such victories in each of the three areas of conflict that we have already considered.

Religious experience, which we took as the type of content incompatible with the dramatic mood, has challenged dramatists from the beginning. Nearly all of these have failed, and most of their successors continue to do so. Hundreds of plays bear witness to the fatal nature of this conflict, either evading the religious experience which they profess to make their subject or, if faithful to their subject, ceasing to be drama at all. But among these hundreds there are a few which have achieved a reconciliation of this content with dramatic form; we can name the *Oresteia*, *Elckerlijc* (translated into English as *Everyman*), *Samson Agonistes*, and *Brand*.[1] This is a slender harvest from two thousand years of dramatic writing and many times this number of plays. But it is remarkable that they should exist at all, and each of them is unforgettable in its power, its nobility, and its originality. Each, moreover, with the possible exception of *Elckerlijc*, creates a modification of existing dramatic form in the process of transmuting its material. To one of these, *Samson Agonistes*,[2] we shall return later, examining more closely with its help the nature and process of this transmutation.

If now we return to our second case, the material which, though natural to epic, cannot be compassed by drama, can we find any plays or groups of plays which overcome the

[1] To these we might add a few which achieve it less fully or in less specific terms, but are, nevertheless, of note; the Brome *Abraham and Isaac*, Shelley's *Prometheus*, the fifth act of *Peer Gynt*, Lunarcharski's *Magi*, Ghéon's *St. Bernard* and T. S. Eliot's *Family Reunion*. The reader will be able to add yet others to this list.

[2] See Chapter II, ' *Samson Agonistes* and Religious Drama '.

apparently insuperable difficulty of scope as *Samson Agonistes*
and *Brand* overcome a seemingly ineradicable antagonism of
mood? We considered that *The Dynasts*, though a great
dramatic poem or epic-drama, could not strictly be called a
great play, because the relation of detail to outline, which
is peculiar to epic, demands a tempo that destroys the concentration peculiar to drama. Is it possible to preserve at
once the concentration of drama and the spaciousness of
epic material? Taken at its face value the question sounds
absurd, and, taken at their face value, the two qualities
appear irreconcilable. But how then can we account for the
sense of vastness, of immense extent and complexity of
factors which is part of our experience in reading the *Oresteia*
or *Antony and Cleopatra* or in recalling the sequence of
Shakespeare's historical plays? Is it possible that Aeschylus
and Shakespeare have found ways of resolving this conflict?
Certainly neither the *Agamemnon* and its companion plays
nor *Antony and Cleopatra* or the individual history plays
lack dramatic concentration or intensity, each in accordance
with its nature. And yet all have in common the power to
impress upon us the magnitude of the issues, the multiplicity
of the lives and events involved. The character list of the
Oresteia is short. How, then, can it convey anything akin to
the multitudinous peopling of epic? *Antony and Cleopatra*
is but a single play. From what source, then, do we gather
the impression of magnitude, of powers reaching and com-
passing the world? The history group is a long tetralogy
with some half-dozen other plays loosely attached at either
end. How, then, although the individual plays are fine
drama in their kind, can there be the necessary coherence of
a sequence, the necessary relation between these parts and
some central matter with which all are concerned? Yet in
all these the double effect remains, the epic spaciousness and
the dramatic concentration.

The means by which this is achieved is clearly different
in each case. It is true that Aeschylus's character-list is
slender; the persons who actually appear are few. But
what of the work done by the chorus, that unique instrument; one of whose many functions is to relate, by reference
to other episodes and other persons, the present with the

past, the immediate with the distant, in ceaseless accompaniment to the action? Does not the sense of the inevitable chain of consequence draw in, as part of our imaginative experience, a host of shadowy figures whose destinies are parts of the cause or parts of the effect of the action that we watch? The action itself is simple, the characters few, but the reverberations are limitless.

It is true, again, that *Antony and Cleopatra* is but a single play and that, long though it is for a play, it would seem absurd to expect the magnitude of scope and extent possible to a poem four times its length. But need it present it directly? Much, it is true, is done even directly, by the widely spaced character grouping and the successive and equally wide changes of scene. But Shakespeare, too, has his instrument at work simultaneously with the direct presentation of the action; in this case it is the imagery which, while it forms a natural part of the speech of his characters, weaves a continuous and independent pattern of its own. And it is to the constant suggestion of this pattern, simultaneously part of and independent of the action, that we owe, in *Antony and Cleopatra*, something of what we owe to the work of choruses in the *Oresteia*.

The problem of Shakespeare's history plays is a different one; the cohesion of epic material has been maintained through a series of independent and self-contained units. It is not enough to say that there is a subject, the glory of England, running through them which is in some sense the theme. That may be true; this theme may serve to link the plays, to give them some special kinship within the body of Shakespeare's work. But it will not serve to preserve the natural relation of the parts of the whole that is characteristic of their material as potential epic. Euripides, for instance, drew all his plays from a few groups of saga material, but we do not for that reason think of the Theban plays as a coherent group, nor those from the Atreus cycle; nor, if the lost plays were recovered to-morrow, should we, I believe, find that they rounded out these groups into artistic wholes. But in Shakespeare's series there is coherence, for there is one central matter with which all are concerned. I say 'matter' rather than 'idea', because in these plays he is concerned more with the relations of man and society as they reveal themselves in the actions of men in public life than with the absolute and speculative questions that held him later. Shakespeare preserves dramatic concentration in the individual plays, especially in those of the central tetralogy, but he affords himself also the spaciousness of epic material in the succession of these and the five supplementary plays, with their numerous characters and events, and the coherence of epic material by slowly building throughout this series a single image to which the central figures of each play bring, as it is written, a contribution that reveals Shakespeare's imaginative exploration of the field. The theme is not the Trojan war or the founding of Rome, but a composite character, the picture of the king or leader, a study of the man best fitted to fill public office, the public man.[1] What finally emerges is not an idea, not an abstraction, but an image as deeply imagined as is the picture which embodies thought in verbal imagery.

Is it possible, finally, to discover a play in which there is a reconciliation of dramatic form with an underlying idea whose nature would seem incompatible with that form, as the complexity of Ibsen's thought proved incompatible in *Emperor and Galilean*? There is at least one notable case in which the dramatist has taken up this challenge in its most direct and uncompromising form. One type of idea is more intractable, more seemingly impossible even than the complexity of thought which we have already noticed—the idea of anarchy itself, the negation of order. If, at any period of his life, a dramatist were for a time to explore this region of thought, to believe chaos and lawlessness to be the ultimate nature of the universe, could he attempt the expression of this interpretation in dramatic form? In abstract terms, in reflective poetry, it could perhaps be compassed, but how achieve the revelation of formlessness in the strict artistic form? The paradox might well seem fantastic and the critic be forgiven who declared that here we reach a borderline beyond which drama cannot go and remain drama. How should the idea of disjunction clothe itself in the compact and clearly articulated form of drama?

[1] See Chapter III, ' Shakespeare's Political Plays '.

Yet this is precisely what one play from Shakespeare's middle period attempts and, I believe, achieves.[1] It was once the fashion to decry *Troilus and Cressida* as a partial failure, and to this day the conflict of mood, matter, and thought, the violent juxtaposition of different textures, may mislead the easy reader into assuming confusion of purpose and breakdown in Shakespeare's art. This is a position from which a deeper reflection forces us to withdraw, and repeated reconsideration of the play in relation to the rest of the Shakespearean sequence leads us instead to the growing conviction that here is no miscarriage of art but an attempt so bold as almost to confound all categories, an achievement of the seemingly impossible.

In the essays which follow I have not attempted to survey the huge field of all dramatic limitation, its causes and possible solution, but to look at a few plays which seem to me to attempt the reconciliation of content and form precisely where it is ' of all things not impossible the most difficult '. I have not been concerned to study the problem so much as the achievement, not the underlying reasons for the conflict, which I have touched on briefly here, but the process by which it is resolved and the nature—so far as I am capable of interpreting it—of the achievement. I have considered Milton's *Samson Agonistes* as a play belonging to the rare category of great religious drama, Shakespeare's history sequence as a group in which epic material is subdued to dramatic form without destruction of the peculiar virtues of either, and his *Troilus and Cressida* as a triumphant revelation of disjunction, of the negation of all order, within the ordered concentration of dramatic shape. Each of these plays achieves what is apparently impossible, pushing forward the limits of drama into territory which, by the very nature of its mood, dimensions or form, seemed forbidden to it. I have then considered some of the technical means by which, in the details of their presentation, dramatists attempt to break down, circumvent or transcend the limitations inherent in dramatic form, the varied functions of dramatic imagery by which ideas and moods may be conveyed more

[1] See Chapter IV, ' Discord in the Spheres : The Universe of *Troilus and Cressida* '.

rapidly and flexibly than in direct presentation of emotion and action ; [1] the technical devices by which the minds and thoughts of the characters are more fully and rapidly revealed than the medium of direct speech will allow.[2] Finally, I have suggested that tragedy itself, the consummation of dramatic art, is held and supported by rigid limitations arising from the demands of its own nature.[3] At bottom it is the same thing that sets the dramatist all his problems. It is the concentration of emotion and tempo, the source of the drama's unique power, that sets him the problem of how to include certain kinds of material. And it is the dramatic medium of direct speech, enhancing this power with its impression of immediacy and actuality, that sets him the problem of how to present it. When without sacrificing concentration or immediacy, he has overcome one or other of the limitations they themselves set up, a great work of art has been created in dramatic form.

[1] See Chapter V, ' The Dramatic Functions of Imagery '.
[2] See Chapter VI, ' The Revelation of Unspoken Thought in Drama '.
[3] See Chapter VII, ' The Equilibrium of Tragedy '.

CHAPTER TWO

SAMSON AGONISTES AND RELIGIOUS DRAMA

MILTON, in his prefatory note to *Samson Agonistes,* made it clear that he regarded his play as a tragedy; but some modern readers do not find it precisely the kind of play that they have been accustomed to call tragedy, either ancient or modern. It ends with the death of Samson, and has a clear technical claim to inclusion in the category. But few of us, if thinking in terms of experience and not of names, are content to call Samson's triumphant death a tragic catastrophe. How could we, indeed, when ' nothing is here for tears '? We are accustomed to associate with tragedy a balance between conflicting moods, between the sense of pain, grief, or terror on the one hand and, on the other, something that triumphs and illuminates. But in Milton's play we find instead a progression towards triumph and illumination which gradually subdues the sense of pain, grief, and loss and at the end transcends and utterly destroys it. Here is clearly something other than the balance of tragedy.[1] Milton oversets the balance in the direction of positive interpretation; by justifying the ways of God to man he leaves no room for tragic ecstasy and substitutes an ecstasy of another kind. He has written, that is, a play that belongs to the rare category of religious drama, a kind which, by the nature of some of its basic assumptions, cannot be tragic.

This distinction between tragedy and religious drama is not a quibble; it goes to the root of the nature of each kind. If it be nearly impossible, as we have already suggested,[2] to subdue the matter of religious experience to the form of drama, it is a frank contradiction in terms to equate religious with tragic experience. The tragic mood is balanced between the religious and the non-religious interpretations of catastrophe and pain, and the form, content, and mood of the

---

[1] Cf. Chapter VII, ' The Equilibrium of Tragedy '.
[2] Chapter I, ' The Limitations of Drama '.

play which we call a tragedy depend upon a kind of equilibrium maintained by these opposite readings of life, to neither of which the dramatist can wholly commit himself.[1]

What, then, are the characteristics of content and form which distinguish religious drama and entitle it to a category of its own? Of what kinds of plays, besides *Samson Agonistes*, do we think when we speak of religious drama, and how has the reconciliation between this apparently irreconcilable content and form been brought about? The first part of this question can perhaps be answered by separating out those plays which have just claim to inclusion from those that, for one reason or another, have none; the second part by considering the play of *Samson Agonistes* itself.

By religious drama I would be understood to mean that kind of drama which takes religious experience for its main theme. It is not, as we have said, a common type; indeed, it is its comparative rarity at all times, and the extreme rareness of great drama of this kind, which first leads us to suspect an inherent incompatibility between drama and the matter of religious experience.[2] The greater part of the material which seems at first glance to claim consideration has no valid claim, and we may well begin by cutting away what is irrelevant.

We may discard first all plays in which religious experience, though touched on or approached, is not the main subject of the action. A play in which a man of apparently saintly life and experience played an incidental part, without his sainthood affecting the lives or actions of the other characters, would not be religious drama, though it might throw some interesting light on the dramatist's convictions or sympathy with such persons. There is every reason to suppose, for instance, that the Abbot with whom Edward II takes refuge is such a man, but we do not for that reason call Marlowe's *Edward II* religious drama. Nor do we in

---

[1] Chapter VII, ' The Equilibrium of Tragedy '.
[2] There is an appearance of paradox here when we remember that, in the few cases in which we can trace the origins of any stream of drama, we find it to have risen in religious ritual. But the paradox vanishes when we notice that the greater part of the drama so derived either rapidly becomes secular, or, if secularisation is delayed, occupies itself with the accompaniments, not the essence of the experience.

the infrequent cases in which such figures appear in Shake-speare's plays. In none of these has the playwright made that figure the centre, nor its experience the main subject of the play. Whether or not he could have done it is beside the point; to have done it he would have had to write a different play, with a different centre and a different theme. At the opposite extreme of the same category is the play of *King Lear*, which contains a series of profound, interrelated studies of conversion. But the religious experience of Lear or of Gloucester is not the main or ostensible subject of the play; it remains among the underlying implications.

This suggestion is quickly despatched, but others require more examination.

There are many plays in which religious practices and habits are assumed as part of the background, and that to such an extent as to affect the action itself. Yet even here we shall, I think, find at least three kinds which we should not, upon reflection, include.

There are, first, those in which characters approach the experience, touch upon it or make play with the idea. Shakespeare's Richard II does this in moments of despond-ency or self-display; but we are hardly tempted to confuse his sentimental religiosity with any form of conversion or complete religious experience. In fact, genuine experience is the one thing we are sure he lacks. This case is unlike our first; we are not here concerned with the presence of genuine religion in a subordinate character, but with some-thing like it but *not* it in the chief character. The Peer Gynt of the fourth act, again, plays in a somewhat different way, with the edges of the experience. But we do not con-fuse his utilitarian and belated attempts at propitiation with religious experience; if the play had stopped there we should not class any part of it as religious drama.

There are, in the second place, certain plays about religious people in which discrimination begins to be more difficult. Here we are asked to accept religious inspiration as the source of the characters' actions and the controlling factor in their behaviour; the subject of the play is the course of action resulting from this inspiration or experience. Are we or are we not to include Mr. Shaw's *Saint Joan* in the group we are trying to compose? I think the answer, for all plays of this kind, will depend upon whether the religious experience is itself the main subject of the play or only the accepted starting point of the action; whether the play is concerned with the process or with the exterior effects. In *Saint Joan* we are clearly concerned with the effects, though, inevitably, as we watch the character in action, we perceive that the process is continuing its work. But we see also that the experience itself is not the theme; the theme is the outward career of the character that it has formed. Even clearer is the case of certain late nineteenth- and early twentieth-century plays in which religion was re-discovered as a dramatic theme. Henry Arthur Jones, in *Saints and Sinners* and *Michael and his Lost Angel*, shows us some of the effects of the experience; but, least of all in the second, a grandiose attempt to dramatize the conflict between the ' world ' and the ' spirit ', do we meet any positive revelation of the experience itself. T. C. Murray, in *Maurice Harte*, has come nearer to it, with his profound understanding of the mental conflict of the young peasant who finds himself committed to the priesthood without vocation. But even he has chosen to reveal the conflict in terms of its effects, and not to make it the actual theme, though, unlike Henry Arthur Jones, he never leaves us in doubt that the experience is real.

There is, in the third place, the deliberate propaganda play, designed to teach the dogma or the ethics of a particular religious system. If we were to include this, we should find our category swelled to enormous bulk, for the whole body of Bible History Plays, Miracle Plays, and Moralities written in Western Europe between the tenth and the sixteenth centuries would immediately enter it. But most of this is ' religious ' only in the most formal sense of the term; it is occupied either with stories taken from the history of the Jews, in which the religious convictions of the characters are an accompaniment rather than the main theme, or with episodes in the life of Christ or of the saints, of which practically the same holds good, or with allegories on the conduct of life that represent the ethical counterparts of the dogmas embodied in both the other kinds. Only very rarely, in an individual play such as the Brome *Abraham and Isaac*, in a single, incidental speech or an isolated conversion scene, do we come upon a direct presentation of religious experience in action.

Finally, before we leave this question of what is *not* religious drama, we must mention certain plays, some of them among the greatest, in which a profound psychological experience is revealed (akin to conversion), without it being certain that the author conceived it as religious.

Ibsen's *The Master Builder*, *Rosmersholm*, and others of his latest group are all plays of conversion, and the conversion is, unlike those in *Lear*, a central part of the mental action of which the play consists. But though some kind of psychological conversion is, in each case, the dominant theme of the play, there is no suggestion that this, like the conversions in *Lear*, has any metaphysical implication. The characters arrive at a greater or less degree of understanding of their own experience; they rid themselves of their illusions, they see what has happened to them and its significance. But they do not (unless in the latest of his plays, which I do not profess as yet to understand) arrive at more than a resolution of their perplexities, a fuller understanding of their relation to the society about them and the underlying moral laws. Their experience does not, apparently, bring them into relation with a spiritual universe from which these moral laws derive. And some perception of the reality of this spiritual universe I should hold to be indispensable in religious experience of any strict mystical kind. If Solness in *The Master Builder* had had the same order of experience as Lear and Gloucester, the play would have been religious drama of a clear kind; if the spiritual experiences of the characters in the play of *Lear* had been made the central theme of the play, as is the psychological development of John Gabriel Borkman, then Lear would, on precisely the same terms, have entered our category.

But there are, I think, a few plays which, as I have suggested,[1] effect a union of the content of religious experience and the form of drama; plays that do not, upon inspection, prove to have evaded the issue by drawing upon

[1] Chapter I, ' The Limitations of Drama '.

some other, related, field.[1] I do not propose to attempt a
comprehensive list, but I would include, as instances to lead
us to the positive issue with which we are concerned, the
Oresteia of Aeschylus, the Brome *Abraham and Isaac*, the
Dutch *Elckerlijc* and its English translation *Everyman*,
Marlowe's *Faustus*, Milton's *Samson Agonistes*, Ibsen's
Brand, and (two out of several representative moderns)
W. B. Yeats' *Hour Glass* and T. S. Eliot's *Family Reunion*.
It is obvious that these are not of equal magnitude and
power, though I think all are at least fine pieces of dramatic
art. But they all have in common one thing, the thing
for which we are looking, the dramatic presentation of
religious experience in one or other of its essential phases.[2]
They do not all offer in equal degree the characteristic
concentration and immediacy of drama, but, though the
structural modifications of some of them are original and even
startling, none of them sacrifices the essentials of dramatic
mood and form. At the same time, whatever the aspect
chosen, the world of experience to which they testify is the
world we find in the writings of St. Augustine, Dante,

---

[1] Since we are concerned here with the art of drama and not with
the literature of religion, I have not considered that interesting body of
plays in the early and the contemporary religious drama of India, in
which fidelity to content is maintained partly at the expense of dramatic
form or of what the European tradition considers dramatic form.

[2] Generally, though not always, the phase chosen is conversion, a
crisis which most readily satisfies the demands of the dramatic mood.
But the plays of conversion are themselves of different kinds. In some
the phases of conversion (or, it may be, of re-conversion) are evenly
distributed throughout the play (as in *Everyman* and *Samson Agonistes*);
in some, the preliminaries are treated at great length and lead us
gradually to the crisis (this is especially so in the *Oresteia*, where the
' conversion ' is less that of an individual than of a society); in one (the
preposterous case of Brand) it is postponed until the last half-line of a
5,000-line play—though its promise has been kept steadily in mind
throughout. In one kindred play, Shelley's *Prometheus*, the process is
consummated well before the end and the subsequent phase of beatitude
occupies the whole of the fourth act, thus attempting to subdue to
dramatic form content associated rather with the music of Beethoven
or the poetry of Dante. One or two plays choose a phase which, even
if not the dramatically obvious one of conversion, is still near the centre
of religious experience. Thus the testing of Abraham's faith (*Abraham
and Isaac*) is nearer to the crisis of martyrdom than to that of conversion. The play is exquisite in its kind, that of the single-episode or
one-act play, but it is hard to imagine this subject supporting the
greater magnitude of a play on the grand scale.

Vaughan, Penn, Bunyan and Blake, in the book of Job and in the Apocalypse. Here, then, if anywhere, we have the paradox of a reconciliation between the experience whose consummation is the resolution of conflict and a form whose power derives from tension and balance.

Can we now draw a few conclusions as to the way in which the reconciliation of matter and form has been made? We notice that all these plays have in common first the choice of religious experience as their main theme, and second the direction the action takes. A dramatic presentation of religious experience is, we find, generally a presentation of the progress into that experience. It may, as in the case of Marlow's *Faustus*, move in a negative direction towards damnation (the religious experience being, if one may venture the paradox, negative), or it may, as in all the other cases, move, at whatever pace the theme demands, towards beatitude. In either case, in so far as it is dramatic, the progress will be through conflict to the victory of one of the contending forces, the religious or the anti-religious, and it must necessarily dwell more upon the emergence than upon the experience, whether of beatitude or damnation, or there will be no conflict strong enough to give dramatic intensity.[1] Since, in practice, religious drama (with the exception of Marlowe's *Faustus*) is almost invariably positive, the only type of conflict that this subject can offer for the use of drama is that of a heroic contest rising to exultation and passing on, in a few rare cases, into beatitude. This is the only point at which this content and this form can be reconciled, and it is at this point that, in all genuine religious drama, the reconciliation has been made. Are we

[1] Only one kind, the victory of the anti-religious forces, could produce tragedy even in the earlier phase of the experience. In fact, Marlowe's *Faustus*, the only example of strict religious drama of this kind that is known to me, almost passes out of the category of tragedy in the negative direction. Marlowe's complete rejection of reconciliation with a beneficent world-order oversets the tragic balance. (See below, Chapter VII, ' The Equilibrium of Tragedy '.) This, of course, does not exclude it from the category of religious drama. But since progression into beatitude cannot, in the nature of things, give us tragedy (even though it may present the technical appearance of a catastrophe in death), we are left in the position of finding no actual example of strict religious drama which is also a balanced tragedy.

now on the way to understand why the drama of religious experience is rare at all times and why the great plays of this kind can be counted almost upon the fingers of one hand ?

We may perhaps draw one more distinction. In some of the plays we have chosen, the contest, though belonging essentially to the domain of the mind, is mirrored in event; a part at least of the character's inner experience is revealed to us in action and not only or mainly by his words. This is true of the *Oresteia* (though Aeschylus could elsewhere use another method), of *Abraham and Isaac*, of *Faustus*, and of *Brand*; all these plays belong to that main division of drama to which event is essential. (*Everyman*, which is an allegorical play, is not strictly of this kind, and the relevant part of *Peer Gynt* (Act V) is perhaps as purely symbolic as *Everyman*.) A notable exception is *Samson Agonistes*, in which the contest takes place entirely in the ' theatre of the soul '. It is a precursor of much modern psychological drama (some of which is also religious in the strict sense) where the inward conflict is revealed directly in the speeches, and the function of event is to occasion or stimulate that progress of the mind which constitutes the real action of the play. It is not necessary to remind either modern readers or good Aristotelians that ' action ' may be a psychological contest with no effect upon the outer world except, possibly, at the end of the play, when the two worlds of thought and event fall together in what is technically the catastrophe; Samson's thought is translated into the act which destroys the Philistines, just as the self-discovery of Rosmer and Rebecca finally transfers itself to the plane of event and cuts off their lives.[1]

---

[1] Although the number of plays in which the action consists in this kind of mental or spiritual contest has grown far greater in the last sixty or seventy years than in the centuries preceding the work of Ibsen, it should be borne in mind that *Samson Agonistes* is, in this respect, as much a descendant of the *Prometheus Vinctus* as a forerunner of *Rosmersholm*. (See for a more detailed comment Chapter II, Section IV, of that fine contribution to the æsthetics of drama, H. D. F. Kitto's recent *Greek Tragedy*.) Certain medieval moralities, again, carry the process to the logical (and undramatic) extreme, which recurs, with the necessary modifications, in a few modern experiments, such as Evreinoff's *Theatre of the Soul*.

But it may be well to remind ourselves that Dr. Johnson thought differently of *Samson Agonistes* and condemned it as having no ' middle ' in Aristotle's sense of the term and so, properly speaking, no action.   He goes through the play [1] looking for a ' well-connected plan ' and finding, to a miracle, the exact opposite of what the modern reader finds : ' At the conclusion of the first act ' (by which he means the end of the ' solemn vindication of divine justice ' in the first choric ode) ' there is no design laid, no discovery made, nor any disposition formed towards the subsequent event.' It ' wants ', that is to say, ' a middle, since nothing passes between the first act and the last that either hastens or delays the death of Samson '.   And ' this is the tragedy which ignorance has admired and bigotry applauded '.

' Ignorance ' and ' bigotry ', in the persons of Jebb, Ker, Bailey and others, to the present day, have continued in various ways—some slightly more subtle than Dr. Johnson's, and revealing a somewhat sounder understanding of the æsthetics of drama—to admire and to applaud. But his view serves well to remind us that the ground on which drama and religion can meet is narrow, so narrow that a genuine union of the two can be misjudged, even in *Samson Agonistes* and even by Dr. Johnson.   The question in dispute between him and the modern critics is whether or not re-ligious (or psychological) experience can constitute the ' action ' of a play. We believe that it can, and so, we may remind ourselves, did Aristotle. But, even as Aristotle's generalizations were unable to take *Hamlet* into consideration, so, it is but just to remember, were Dr. Johnson's unable to take in *Rosmerholm*.

May we, then, once again consider *Samson Agonistes*, and now as a play whose ' action ' consists not only in a mental progress (akin on one side to the *Prometheus* of Aeschylus and on the other to *John Gabriel Borkman*), but in a progress of a particular kind, drawn from material that is normally, by the nature of its emotion, compatible with drama only within narrow limits yet here shaped into dramatic form.

---

[1] Rambler, 139–140. The observations made in these two essays are supported, but not extended, in the brief references in the *Life of Milton*.

C

We shall, that is to say, trace moods, phases, and states of mind instead of actions (of which, as Dr. Johnson pointed out, there are none until the end). If the play is what we have supposed it to be, these moods will be causally related as events are related in a finely built drama of action, and there will be a psychological beginning, middle, and end as plain to trace as in the plot of *Macbeth*. And all this will be achieved within the narrow limits left to drama when it embodies religious experience and to religious experience when it takes on dramatic form.

The mood of the opening speeches appears to be the motion-less inertia of despair. There is no hope; not even con-tinuity of thought. Samson's mind is, like his body, ' care-lessly diffus'd '. Were it not for the ' restless thoughts that rush upon (him) thronging ', there would not even be the promise of action. In effect the inertia is not absolute or the despair complete, for there are periods of sustained bitter-ness, rebellious impulses that show a fitful power. There is also an intermittent effort to trace detachedly the causes of the disaster; a survival of the habit of disciplined thought. But when the chorus enters there are still, as it were, but the unassembled elements of a mind; inertia and despair, if not absolute, prevail. This, and what immediately follows, may fairly be said to constitute a beginning.

The first choric speech, unheard by Samson, has an import-ant dramatic function, both arousing the sympathies of the audience and enriching their knowledge (or memories) of the past and its contrast with the present. But these, though necessary, are subsidiary functions, part of the exposition of the play, and the action proper only begins with their address to Samson (l. 178). The chorus (like most visitations of friends from the time of Job downwards) soon falls into the question, Why did you do it? and calls up the superb, frank egoism of Samson, which had already appeared at intervals, in a passage of self-justification (l. 241 *seq.*). This leads immediately to the lines (293 *seq.*) in which the chorus, ceasing to be interlocutors, take on another function and reveal, in a debate on the justice of God, the thought that is in Samson's mind. The doubt that had lain unexpressed since the beginning is admitted and, if not resolved, at least rebutted, and a main cause of division in the mind is weakened. It is from this point, I think, that that unification of the mind which is a necessary preliminary to any action begins.

Milton wastes no time, but immediately brings in Manoa. Manoa enters lamenting, and we know that for the purposes of the action he could not have done a better thing. For the lament rouses Samson to defend the decrees of Heaven and to lay the blame steadily upon himself. The timing of this is exquisite. The lamentations would have been useless before the slight tonic effects of the choric dialogue had worked upon Samson's mind, and perhaps no other impact would have served the same purpose as they do, following immediately upon that dialogue. The quality and kind of stimuli that Milton applies to Samson's mind are like a highly skilled course of psychotherapy : each comes at its due moment, before which it would have been overpowering and after which inadequate. We are in the hands of a man who knows this experience intimately and of an artist who can assemble the raw material of life into form. Event, even minor event, such as Manoa's visit, serves simply to stimulate that mental progress which is the action. The sole function of event is thus, until the climax of the play, to produce thought or emotion, not, as in the drama of action, to reveal them. Samson's mind moves forward a necessary stage on its journey because Manoa—or Harapha or Dalila —visits him; by the way he receives each successively he reveals the stage to which the last has brought him. Only at the end does his mind show itself in action and event cease to function solely as the cause and become simultaneously the result of thought.

The inspired blunders of Manoa serve the same purpose throughout. The news of the feast of Dagon, which a little earlier in the play would have led to despair, falls upon a mind now capable of being roused by the challenge ' So Dagon shall be magnified ', to draw a distinction between his fortunes and those of the God of his worship. Despairing for and still condemning himself, he perceives, in a sudden leap of the mind forward, the power of God to accomplish His own purposes (' God doth not need either man's work or his own gifts '). A preliminary climax, a foretaste of exultation is reached.

> This only hope relieves me, that the strife
> With me hath end; all the contest is now
> 'Twixt God and Dagon; Dagon hath presum'd
> Me overthrown, to enter lists with God,
> His Deity comparing and preferring
> Before the God of *Abraham*. (460–5.)

As Manoa (whose mind, like that of Dr. Johnson's, interprets Samson's story in terms of events and not of inner experience) suggests alternative means of escape from his bondage, Samson's vision grows proportionately clearer and he distinguishes more sharply the life of the mind from the subsidiary life of the body. From this point onward Milton makes it plain that the death of the body will never be more than an incident in Samson's life, the significant episodes disengaging themselves more and more clearly.

> All otherwise to me my thoughts portend,
> That these dark orbs no more shall treat with light,
> Nor th' other light of life continue long
> But yield to double darkness now at hand :

The impulse then exhausts itself and the action seems as if it will go no further. Indeed, without fresh stimulus from event, it might end on the note ' God of our Fathers, what is man ', the challenge that shows Milton's bitter knowledge of the dark night of the spirit that he seems here for the first time to understand.[1] But just as, when the movement of a normal drama of action appears to flag, an episode, arising naturally from the circumstances of the plot, may turn the whole accumulated force into a fresh channel, so here, the entry of Dalila rallies the momentarily flagging force of the play and sends it triumphantly to its conclusion. For Dalila brings a different and fiercer conflict, sterner than the disputes (themselves of steadily increasing force) with the

---

[1] One of the most surprising qualities of *Samson Agonistes* is this, that Milton, who could write *Paradise Lost* without any indication of mystical experience, in this play suddenly associates himself with those who have made strong, original contributions to the records of the experience and the analysis of its phases.

chorus and with Manoa. She provokes Samson to wrath
and self-determination. She concentrates his imagination
not upon the heroic part of his miscarried glory, but on the
matter-of-fact, the practical, the petty, everyday things that
have deflected the currents of the mind. He grows more
alert, he puts out more strength; this victory costs more
than the earlier ones. And as she engages him closer and
closer we notice how severely logical is the argument (even
Dr. Johnson gave Milton due credit for this), how nobly
clear and sustained the survey over their past as they
uncover layer by layer the conduct and motives that brought
it about.[1] Even in the exultation of Dalila's last speech
this quality remains. Then, its work done, the work of
disciplining and welding together the faculties of Samson,
the episode ends and leaves him lifted above even that
degree of self-despair which had remained, roused by anger
and disciplined by logic into a mood resolute and ready for
inspiration.

The dialogue with Harapha makes clear how far the last
episode has advanced the action. Samson's speech reveals
the active presence of certain moral qualities; courage, self-
respect, self-control, faith, and the intellectual virtue of
disciplined and ordered thought. The restoration of these
we have traced step by step through the earlier episodes.
The conflict with Harapha, which is the direct result of the
state of mind into which he has been brought, now transfers a
part of the action to the plane of event; what had been purely
psychological action begins to express itself simultaneously
in thought and in deeds. But it has still some steps further
to go. From the exit of Harapha the mind of Samson
enters upon a phase in which it is resolute, clear, and steady.
The process of rehabilitation is complete and energy of spirit
and power of continuous thought return. From now onward
Samson's speech, and that of the chorus which echoes him,
is illuminated with prophetic flashes of exultation. It still
needs the first visit of the Philistian officer to assemble them
and give them direction. The heroic contest is completed;

---

[1] This is a delightful anticipation of the method used with supreme
art by Ibsen in *Rosmersholm* and extended in details (though not in
essentials) by Pirandello in our own day.

exultation takes possession, and from this moment the play
sweeps up easily to the triumphant climax :

> Be of good courage, I begin to feel
> Some rowzing notions in me which dispose
> To something extraordinary my thoughts. . . .
> If there be ought of presage in my mind,
> This day will be remarkable in my life. . . .

It is to be noticed that the accident of physical death
(which, if we read the action of the play in terms of its
events, is the catastrophe) is clearly separated now in
Samson's mind from significant experience. It is hardly
important, one way or the other :

> Happen what may, of me expect to hear
> Nothing dishonourable, impure, unworthy
> Our God, our Law, my Nation or myself,
> The last of me or no, I cannot warrant.

From this point onward the outward events bear the impress
of this exultation achieved through contest, and, despite the
ironic relief of Manoa's speeches before the death of Samson,
the play passes on undisturbed to the mood of beatitude
which is the natural conclusion of religious drama :

> All is best, though we oft doubt
> What th' unsearchable dispose
> Of highest wisdom brings about,
> And ever best found in the close.

There is, then (*pace* Dr. Johnson, of whom we may now
take leave), a profound and dramatic psychological contest
in this play, and, if it be not ' action ', it is difficult to apply
that term to much of the major drama of the Greeks and of
the moderns. The earlier episodes of the play do not merely
illustrate or reveal but cause that progress of the mind which
is the real theme, and the final episodes mutually cause and
are caused by it.[1] The severest dramatic economy is
revealed in the ordering of both, and the play is as strict and
unified a work of art as any we could examine.

[1] If this does not constitute ' a beginning, a middle and an end ',
it is difficult to say what a middle is. It is perhaps when we misuse the
term ' tragedy ' that we are liable to misplace the emphases (especially
upon the death of Samson), and find ourselves complaining with Dr.
Johnson that the middle part of the play does not further the end and
so is no Aristotelian ' middle '.

If this be a just conclusion, we shall find this unity revealed in every aspect of the play which we can study. Since a great work of art is an organism and not an amplification of a schematic design, we shall find the main theme revealed and interpreted not only by the ordering of the episodes and their variations of tension and pace; the relations of the characters, the accompanying commentary, the prosody and the imagery will also show continuity, a progression reflecting that of the main movement. For it is a distinctive mark of a great work of art that each of these would itself—isolated, if that were possible, from all the others—offer a rendering of the main theme and of the essential mood of the play. Since we are concerned here with a play in which one of the most notable limitations of drama is transcended, it is perhaps worth while to remind ourselves to what extent it has that organic nature which is characteristic of a great work of art. Can we perhaps indicate something of this by looking in a little more detail at one of these other aspects?

To many readers, the prosody of *Samson Agonistes*, the musical technique which carries so easily the bold, almost arrogant, variations, a technique as supreme as Shakespeare's later prosody, is more satisfying than that of any other phase of Milton's work. This alone would suggest that the play was a fully harmonized work of art, and this suggestion is confirmed when we see that the prosodic form of the play is itself a living organism. The play is a sustained, continuous musical composition, the parts resiliently related each to each and to the whole, and can no more be understood prosodically than logically if it is only considered line by line; the one aspect offers a texture as seamless as the other.

The progressive modulations of the verbal music are, that is, an aspect of the psychological progression that forms the main theme,[1] passing from the rhythms of flat, inert despair, through those of restless conflict and turmoil to the clear, hard movement of argument, or, again, through the swinging,

---

[1] I shall not attempt here to analyse the details of the effect; the relation in individual lines of verbal music and meaning has been examined by Bridges. I am only attempting to indicate the outlines of the musical composition referred to above.

marked rhythms of exultation into the level verse of serenity,
plain and relatively unvaried.

This can be demonstrated in some detail,[1] though even a
sketch of the musical form of the play does but scant justice
to that form, which reveals itself as a series of exquisitely
related curves in sculptural design.   As in all great poetic
drama, the prosodic form of *Samson Agonistes* can constitute
an experience complete in itself, a reinterpretation of the
main theme in terms of verbal music.   The dramatic function
of the imagery [2] is akin to that of the prosody.   For it also
follows, reflects, and reinterprets in another medium the
experience which is the theme of the play.   This consonance,
this close relating of all the aspects of its technique with the
main design, is a sure sign—if we needed signs to convince
us—that the play is a living organism, no sterile and artificial
product, but a major work of art.

The form of *Samson Agonistes*, then, whether we consider
the relation of episodes and the general shaping of the play
or the progression revealed in the similarly related prosody
and imagery, is peculiar to its kind.   The theme of religious
experience when, as is rare, it takes dramatic form, appears to
follow certain broad lines of action, and these themselves
determine the form in general and in detail.   Milton's play
is no miscarried tragedy, but a major work of this rare, but
distinctive kind, among the finest of that kind in our experience.   The doubt whether it is a living work of art, the doubts
as to its formal soundness, falter when we realize the firm
lines with which the theme is developed; the steady psychological progression from despair through heroic conflict
upwards to exultation and the final assumption into beatitude; the unerring reflection of this in the relation of the
episodes each to each and to the main theme, in the steady
development in tempo and tension, and in the simultaneous
and equivalent progression in imagery and prosody.   It is
not the formal weakness, but the formal wholeness of the
play that astounds us.   Seldom was an artistic experience
more unfalteringly sustained and more clearly communicated.
The hesitations of certain critics are perhaps due in part to

[1] See Appendix, p. 148.
[2] Cf. also Chapter V, ' The Functions of Imagery in Drama '.

their attempts to judge it as tragedy, but probably more to the attempt to judge it by criteria of form and construction based on our experience of the more familiar kinds of drama.

For, as has been indicated in this essay, this specific content determines for itself a special form, and often dispenses with event and outward action to substitute a progression of inward crises or phases of mood causally related and leading to their own resolution. If this resolution is simultaneously imaged on the plane of action, by death or some other apparent outward catastrophe, it is possible to regard the play as an intended but miscarried tragedy, and to point out that the earlier phases do not lead naturally to the catastrophe. What is overlooked in this view is that the apparent catastrophe is as purely subsidiary to the real action as is (for example) commentary in the final phases of the drama of event. The earlier phases do not lead consistently towards it because it is not, in itself, the significant climax of the action. What they do lead to (and this often with consummate skill in architectural grace and solidity) is the resolution of the spiritual conflict which the apparent catastrophe serves only to image in terms of event.

CHAPTER THREE

SHAKESPEARE'S POLITICAL PLAYS

IN the sequence of the history plays, Shakespeare, as I have suggested in an earlier chapter,[1] achieved a reconciliation of epic material with dramatic form, somewhat as Milton, in *Samson Agonistes*, transmuted the matter of religious experience into drama. In studying Milton's play, we were drawn imperceptibly into describing its dramatic power; for the reality of the religious experience was self-evident, and the question whether or not the reconciliation had been achieved rested upon that of whether or not the resulting work was dramatic. With Shakespeare's histories we find ourselves, equally of necessity, approaching from the opposite direction. We do not, at this point in Shakespeare studies, question whether individual plays are dramatic, but we may well question whether or not the series contains the material of epic. We may perhaps suggest in what ways and by what means they have preserved the spaciousness and coherence of their epic material as well as the concentration and immediacy of drama.[2]

The spaciousness has been preserved by the fact that we have primarily a group of four central plays supported by at least four or five more (one of which is of unquestioned dramatic power), extending together over several historical periods and introducing some two hundred different characters. This, of course, does not in itself guarantee the effect of vastness; it might merely guarantee chaos. But the balance and relating of characters in Shakespeare's hands are such that we experience the multifariousness of life and not mere confusion. The presence of some element of continuity between the plays of the main and even of the subsidiary group[3] is, I think, less obvious; but it is this

[1] See Chapter I, ' The Limitations of Drama '.

[2] I have endeavoured to observe here, as in Chapter I, the customary distinction between ' epic material ' and ' epic '.

[3] The group of plays with which we are mainly concerned here is the series *Richard II*, *Henry IV* (1 and 2) and *Henry V*, for in these four the simultaneous effect of epic space and dramatic concentration

which ultimately gives coherence to the wealth of material.
In fact, it is precisely here that the challenge of epic form to
dramatic material arises. For a series of plays on related
themes, with a certain number of overlapping characters,
though clear and ordered in their individual disposal of their
material, might yet remain no more than a number of excellent individual works of art, illuminating each other, but
affording no continuous and coherent image, no central,
emergent idea. Now, in most epic material we find a central
figure, some aspect of whose life and experience forms a
theme to which, should an epic poem be written upon that
subject, everything in the poem could be made to contribute. Each character, episode, or group of events could
bear, that is, a necessary relation to this central figure or
idea, illuminating and illuminated by it, while at the same
time maintaining its own relation, in the spatial and chronological scheme of the poem, with the other characters,
episodes, and events. Aeneas's wanderings are a naturally
shaped sequence, and can be causally related in a work of
art, provided that all that is included affects or illuminates
his experience and purpose.

This complete cohesion is characteristic only of the epic
itself; there is, as a rule, only potential cohesion in the raw
epic material. But is there anything akin to this potential

---

may be most clearly observed. But the gradually built-up figure of
the king, which gives significance and unity to this central group, is
supported by the exploration and commentary of the four earlier plays,
and by various studies of kings and statesmen in the later. Accordingly,
I have sometimes drawn upon these also for their contributions, whether
as a preliminary group whose significant order is that of the writing,
or as subsequent observations and conclusions revealing the implications of the main group. There is a certain apparent inconsistency in
deriving the union of epic magnitude and dramatic concentration
partly from the earlier group of plays for which (with the exception
of *Richard III*) we cannot claim the highest dramatic quality, and partly
again from several detached later plays for which we cannot claim
continuity of subject. But it is more apparent than actual; the
contributions of the three earlier plays are almost entirely in the form
of negative conclusions and the substance of their findings recapitulated
in the main group, while those of the later plays are a revaluation of
the central image of that same group. The service of both to the
present argument is that of revealing explicitly what is included by
implication in the main, and central, group, and thus permitting it to
be stated more briefly and with fewer qualifications.

continuity of epic material in the series of Shakespeare's
political plays? Can we distinguish in them something
which relates what would else be isolated units, causing them
to illuminate each other and to contribute, each in turn, some
indispensable part of a whole whose balance would be
impaired without it?

I think we can distinguish some such factor in Shakespeare's series, but, as I have suggested,[1] it will not be found
in the generally prevailing mood of nationalism (and his
attitude to nationalism passes through many phases between
the writing of *Henry VI* and the writing of *Henry V*) nor in
any single character.[2] The central and continuous image in
these plays, more specific than a mood, more comprehensive
than a character, is, I believe, a composite figure—that of
the statesman-king, the leader and public man, which
Shakespeare builds up gradually through the series of the
political plays from *Henry VI* to *Henry V*. This figure
recurs, in varying forms, through the greater part of Shakespeare's drama, for after the picture is completed in the
political plays he appears to revise and reconsider it, studying
it from a different angle in several of the tragedies and late
plays. For the purposes of this discussion we are concerned
with the political plays, and chiefly with those four in which
Shakespeare achieves simultaneously the abundance of epic
material and the cogency of drama. But I have permitted
myself, in order to indicate the vastness and complexity of
this image, to include some evidence of his later thought;
the revaluation, by reason of which he builds up a con-
trasting portrait, thereby making explicit and definite what
had been implicit in that first portrait with which we are
primarily concerned.

The portrait of the statesman-king is the result of a series
of explorations, now the study of a failure, now of a partial
success; a vast, closely articulated body of thought imaged
always in terms of actual character, yet completely incor-
porated in no one character. The figure that finally emerges

[1] Chapter I.
[2] Methuselah and the Flying Dutchman apart, obviously no character
could hope to begin as the contemporary of John and end as that of
Richard III.

is not Falconbridge or Theseus or Henry IV or Henry V,
yet it would be incomplete if any one of them were taken
away; nor is it the mere opposite of Henry VI or John or
Richard III or Richard II, yet it would also be incomplete
if one of these were destroyed.   These separate images are
but statements or qualifications contributing to that vaster
image, no one of them in itself coextensive with the composite
whole.   It is this which gives coherence to the material of
the history plays, which nevertheless remain individual
works of art.   If it is true that Shakespeare has thus subdued
potential epic material to dramatic form, may we now consider in more detail certain plays, in order to see how the
emergent figure of the king dominates and draws to itself the
whole of the central series ?

Of the figures who appear in Shakespeare's political plays,
we need survey only a certain group—the men upon whom
the highest offices devolve.   Inevitably, with an Elizabethan
or Jacobean writer, this means the office of kingship, or of
leadership in some form very like kingship.   The position
may be reached by violence and usurpation or by peaceful
inheritance; in the first place the man may be capable of
maintaining it and so partly justified in his action, or incapable of what he attempts, and so lose it; in the second
case he may lend himself willingly to the task or it may be
thrust upon an unwilling or an inadequate man.   But in
every case, from his earliest to his latest work, Shakespeare
makes an imaginative exploration of the experience, adding
something to the vast body of his comment on the figure of
the statesman-king.   Moreover, he is, broadly speaking, concerned in his Elizabethan phase mainly with what the office
requires in the man, in his Jacobean phase with what the office
does to the man.   He passes, that is, from an interest centred
chiefly in building up the picture of an ideal king or leader, to
a study of the effect on the individual of the demands and
privileges of his office.

Shakespeare's first explorations of this field seem to have
been incidental to other work and to have led him, for the
most part, to negative conclusions.   The process by which
he feels his way towards the centre of the experience is
familiar to all his readers.   The figure of Henry VI is the

first which he is forced to consider (and at this early stage there presumably was an element of compulsion in the choice of the theme), and by his way of portraying the disasters of that reign Shakespeare shows clearly that he perceives some element of kingliness to be lacking. Henry is a pious, reflective man, by no means lacking in dignity, with a conscientious, but not necessarily intelligent, sense of his position. In an age when kings must be equally competent in peace and war, he is too simple for a politician (much less a statesman) and too ready to trust to conciliation to be a soldier. He lets his wife and his supporters fight his battle while he sits upon a hill alongside the field and laments that he has not been born a shepherd; yet at his death he claims in all good faith that he has loved his people and is convinced that they have no cause to desert him. A good man, a conscientious man, admirably suited for certain kinds of private, or, better still, monastic life; but neither firm, intelligent, shrewd, nor capable. A figure that tells us clearly that Shakespeare has already marked and inwardly digested the admonitions of the 7th chapter of Machiavelli's *Prince* and sees that ruthlessness is sometimes merciful and that a ' dangerous lenity ' has no place among the ' king-becoming graces '.

Nor, for the matter of that, has a pure self-seeking individualism, and this type of leader he unhesitatingly despatches at the end of *Henry VI* and in the course of *Richard III*. What may be briefly termed the Tamburlaine–Hotspur–Essex–Byron figure that fascinated Chapman, the great lawless sixteenth-century nobleman whose purpose was his own glorification, had short shrift at Shakespeare's hands. Actually, Richard III receives less consideration as a type of leader than almost any other figure. He stands, in the group of Shakespeare's kings, as a crude but highly coloured specimen of the Tudor adventurer, storming his way to power, possessing the kingdom by violence, but unstable both on account of the violence of his passion and of some weakness inherent in the act of usurpation itself.

Indeed, it is this attitude of possessiveness that Shakespeare seems next to notice as one at least of the factors in the downfall of many leaders, and, as he defines it more clearly in *King John*, there forms behind it the shadowy suggestion of an opposite quality which comes, in the end, to be the essence of Shakespeare's positive ideal of kingship. The kings and rulers in *King John* all talk of their countries in terms of possession; the country is their property, they are landlords whose responsibilities go no further than treating it well enough to get a good yield from it; being men of sense, they preserve or protect it so that it does not depreciate, but there is no glimmer in their minds of any other feeling. Only in the mind of Salisbury, which misgives him at the thought of bringing civil war among the people he should protect, and in that of Falconbridge, who sees that the king is responsible for putting courage and good heart into his people, is there anything further. In Falconbridge we have a positive, if simple, ideal of service, a positive picture of kingly bearing and, incidentally, certain attributes that reappear in all Shakespeare's later successful kings; tenacity, resourcefulness, and shrewdness.

It is at this point that Shakespeare pauses to sum up, in a somewhat unexpected place, the positive findings of these first four political plays. The findings have, we admit, been up to now mainly negative—it is easier to write dramatically about disastrous reigns than about calm and prosperous ones, and there were more on record in the late sixteenth century. A king must not be submissive, conciliatory, and retiring (like Henry VI), however pious and conscientious; still less must he be a self-indulgent sentimentalist like Edward IV. But neither must he be a marauding egotist like Richard III, nor a landlord of his country like John, Philip, and the King of Austria. All these bring disaster with them and themselves end in disaster, because, however else they may differ, they are all at bottom individualists who have not sunk their individualism in their office of leader. It matters little to Shakespeare, at this stage and in this connexion, whether the individualism take the form of withdrawal from the world or of rapacious assault upon it, whether the natural habitat of the mind be a monastery or a battlefield. Both alike fail to meet the demands of sixteenth-century kingship because they do not think primarily of their office as a demand.

And it is here that the other figure to which I referred is interposed, that short study of a king who is indeed kingly; firm, just, even-tempered, possessed of a broad humanity and the characteristic Tudor love of his people, which, while it will no longer regard them as counters in an international gamble, yet knows precisely how to make a discreet display of that humanity and that love, so as to rivet unshakably the affections of those people. In the consciousness of the political value of these affections, no less than in the already slightly cynical realization of the manipulation needed to keep them at their height, Shakespeare has made a long step forward from the group of early historical plays.

The. What are they that do play it?
Phil. Hard-handed men, that work in Athens here,
Which never labour'd in their minds till now;
And now have toiled their unbreathed memories
With this same play, against your nuptial.
The. And we will hear it.
. . . What poor duty cannot do, noble respect
Takes it in might, not merit.
Where I have come, great clerks have purposed
To greet me with premeditated welcomes;
Where I have seen them shiver and look pale,
Make periods in the midst of sentences,
Throttle their practis'd accent in their fears,
And, in conclusion, dumbly have broke off,
Not paying me a welcome. Trust me, sweet,
Out of this silence yet I pick'd a welcome:
And in the modesty of fearful duty
I read as much as from the rattling tongue
Of saucy and audacious eloquence.

This, it may well be contended, is not Theseus speaking, but, rather, a greater than Theseus, the last and greatest of the Tudor monarchs, who had ' the heart of a king and of a king of England, too '. But, what is equally significant for our purpose, it is already an anticipation of one of the dominant voices from the next group of plays, the group of the major histories, whose task is to build up the positive figure of kingship, to which the group of minor and preliminary histories have so far contributed only negative suggestions. The ground, then, has been thoroughly cleared by the time Shakespeare reaches the great tetralogy (*Richard II*, *Henry IV*, I and II, *Henry V*), and a few positive suggestions have been made.

The portrait of Richard II defines more clearly what is already implied, the fatal weakness of self-indulgent egotism, even though it be accompanied by private graces or virtues. But it adds, far more strongly, a picture of the fatal blindness that arrogates to itself the privileges of kingship while disregarding the responsibilities on whose account alone the privileges exist. Shakespeare's effective leaders, Falconbridge, Theseus, Henry IV, Henry V, Claudius, all see with perfect clearness the essential reciprocity of these two, and the last three at least have no sentimental illusions about either. Richard, in whom the sense of privilege amounts to megalomania, serves to define the extreme of that position, just as his immediate successor, Henry IV, defines the extreme position of the man oppressed by the sense of responsibility. (Here, as in so much else, it is Henry V who achieves the balance and reconciliation of the two.)

> Not all the water in the rough rude sea
> Can wash the balm from an anointed king;
> The breath of worldly men cannot depose
> The deputy elected by the Lord :
> For every man that *Bolingbroke* hath pressed,
> To lift shrewd steel against our golden crown,
> God for his *Richard* hath in heavenly pay
> A glorious angel. Then, if angels fight,
> Weak men must fail, for Heaven still guards the right.

But Richard, with his extravagant claims, serves a further purpose. His half-inspired, half-insane religiosity sees in the holder of his office the immediate representative of God on earth, claims for the king a consequent divinity, and genuinely believes that the hosts of Bolingbroke will fall before the ' glorious angels ' whom ' God for his Richard hath in heavenly pay '. That there is something in what he says Shakespeare never, either at this time or before or after it, denies. In this particular play the very difficulty of dislodging Richard from the throne indicates it clearly, and in the earlier play we find that Henry VI is equally difficult to remove, while the courageous and astute Richard of Gloucester maintains his balance only with great difficulty and for a short time. There *is* something sacred in inheritance, and, though the evidence of the early plays has all

D

pointed to the forming of this idea, it is in *Richard II* that, at a touch, it suddenly crystallizes out. Henry VI and Richard II, in their different ways inadequate men, have strong titles; and an unflawed title, if not half the king, is at least an important part of him. It is at least difficult to ' wash the balm from an anointed king ' though it may not— and indeed does not—need ' all the water in the rough rude sea ' to do it.

But if this hectic religiosity, this inflated claim of divine right, is fantastic in Richard's mouth, it is no longer fantastic when it haunts the broken dreams of the dying Henry IV. For the character and position of Henry IV introduce a set of problems the exact opposite of those of Richard II and new in Shakespeare's survey. Henry, fine statesman and excellent ruler as he is, is crippled and frustrated by his flawed title, and the sense of the sacredness of inheritance is as strong in him, who was perpetually reminded of his lack of it, as it ever was in Richard, and is accompanied by a far shrewder estimate of its significance.

The solution of the problems of the two parts of *Henry IV* and *Henry V* is the peculiar contribution of Shakespeare's Elizabethan phase to the summation of his idea of a king, of the man who should fit at every point the demands laid upon him by public office. Henry IV has all the qualities necessary to a king and avoids all the weaknesses of temperament in the portrayal of which the positive qualities have, so far, been implied. He has shrewdness, tenacity, and self-command that already approaches self-concealment; he has the true Tudor sense of the value of discreet popularity. He is as astute as a badger and has very much the same tough courage. He is not self-indulgent, he is not vain, he is not self-absorbed. He is not even a saint or a poet. He is an exceedingly able, hard-working statesman whose career reveals gradually but clearly the main qualification for kingship, the king's sense of responsibility to his people, that sense of service which, while making him no more than the state's greatest servant, makes all his privileges and exemptions, even a measure of autocracy itself, no more than necessary means for that service. Domineering he is, at times, like Shakespeare's prototype of Tudor monarchy, but he has, in the main, decent intentions, and he possesses, through thick and thin, an unfailing, humorous sense of proportion.

Having, then, such potentialities, why is he not the final figure in the group? The answer is obvious after the study of *Richard II*. The flaw in Henry's title, the fatal act of usurpation with which Richard had made such fine play, does indeed cripple his power and, through that, his mental stature, eating into his confidence and bringing down all loftiness of gesture or intention to the necessity of cunning and circumspection. Character no less than tenure suffers thus under the nemesis for an outrage done to the sacredness of inheritance. Henry IV is in nearly all things a potential Henry V and, trembling upon the verge of achievement, he looks into the promised land, and, as so often happens, speaks more explicitly of it than those who have dwelt in it familiarly. That is why it is, I think, impossible to understand Henry V as Shakespeare saw him, the Henry V who never speaks out, unless we can see his position and his intentions through the eyes of Bolingbroke's frustration :

> Heaven knows, my son,
> By what by-paths, and indirect, crook'd ways
> I met this crown : and I myself know well
> How troublesome it sat upon my head.
> To thee, it shall descend with better quiet,
> Better opinion, better confirmation :
> For all the soil of the achievement goes
> With me, into the earth.

It is left to Henry V to gather up in himself all that is fitting and necessary to a king and to remain as the epitome of the Elizabethan idea of the ' politicke vertues '. Shakespeare has at last resolved his demands upon such a figure into certain clearly defined qualifications and summed them all in Henry V, with his unflawed, hereditary title and his assured possession of all kingly attributes. With his broad-based popularity, his genuine love of public service for its own sake, his strong sense of responsibility, and his equally clear sense of its relation to privilege, his shrewd statesman's brain, successfully masked as that of a simple soldier, he stands where, perhaps, no king in drama has stood before or after him. Church and state, commoners and noblemen, soldiers and civilians, he knows them all, with a knowledge

rooted in the taverns of Eastcheap, and holds them in his
hand, too practised, popular, and secure to make a show of
mastery. He was a statesman fulfilling Burke's demand—
he knew how the whole world lived. He was a monarch,
modelled upon the greatest of the Tudors, Elizabeth herself.
It probably happens to every man to believe, at one time or
another, for a time at least, that the greatest of the arts is
conduct. And it is some such experience as this, in Shakespeare's career, that lies, I think, at the base of the great
historical studies culminating in the figure of Henry V.

But if this were all, the composite figure would be shorn
of half its subtlety and magnitude. We are aware already
in this play that Shakespeare has gone beyond the experience he is primarily describing; that, implicit in this carefully balanced study, this culmination of so long and careful
an exploration, is the germ of some later revulsion of thought
which refutes it, as the great destructive speeches of Timon
refute Ulysses' speech on the beauty of degree, of the ordered
hierarchical state. For a while, it may be, between the
writing of *Henry IV* and *Henry V*, Shakespeare believed
the highest achievement of man to be the ordered state
he afterwards described in *Troilus and Cressida*, the image
of the ordered universe, of the cosmos with its regulated
spheres.

> The Heavens themselves, the planets, and this centre,
> Observe degree, priority, and place,
> Insisture, course, proportion, season, form,
> Office, and custom, in all line of order : . . .
>   But when the planets
> In evil mixture to disorder wander,
> What plagues, and what portents, what mutiny ?
> What raging of the sea ?   Shaking of earth ?
> Commotion in the winds, frights, changes, horrors,
> Divert and crack, rend and deracinate
> The unity and married calm of states
> Quite from their fixture ?   O, when degree is shak'd,
> (Which is the ladder to all high designs)
> The enterprise is sick.   How could communities,
> Degrees in schools, and brotherhoods in cities,
> Peaceful commerce from dividable shores,
> The primogenitive and due of birth,
> Prerogative of age, crowns, sceptres, laurels,
> (But by degree) stand in authentic place ?
> Take but degree away, untune that string,
> And hark what discord follows.

The keystone of this order was the figure of the perfect public man, of Henry V. All the implications of the foregoing plays point to this ultimate emergence of the complete figure. In all the anticipations that lead up to him, and particularly in the later scenes of the second part of *Henry IV*, Shakespeare has, he would seem to imply, ' in this rough work, shaped out a man '; the great art of conduct, and of public conduct at that, is at last truly understood.

But has he? Or has he, as it were unawares, and led already on to some perception beyond his immediate purpose, shaped out instead something that is at once more and less than a man. Henry V has indeed transformed himself into a public figure; the most forbidding thing about him is the completeness with which this has been done. He is solid and flawless. There is no attribute in him that is not part of this figure, no desire, no interest, no habit even that is not harmonized with it. He is never off the platform; even when, alone in a moment of weariness and of intense anxiety, he sees with absolute clearness the futility of privilege and the burden of responsibility, he still argues his case in general terms, a king's life weighed against a peasant's, peasant against king. No expression of personal desire escapes him; though he makes almost the same comparison as Henry VI, he is detached alike from king and shepherd, commenting upon them, but wasting no more strength on imagining what cannot be than on deluding himself, like Richard, with the empty glories of his state. He has inured himself so steadfastly to the life of a king, lived so long in councils and committees, weighing, sifting, deciding, commanding, that his brain automatically delivers a public speech where another man utters a cry of despair, of weariness or of prayer. It is in vain that we look for the personality of Henry behind the king; there is nothing else there. We know how his brain works upon any one of half a dozen problems; the treachery of Cambridge, Grey, and Scroop, the fomenting of wars abroad to preserve peace at home, the disaffection in the army, the difficulties of a formidable campaign, and the equally great dangers of a crushing victory. We see the diplomacy, the soldiership, the vigilant, astute eye upon the moods of people and barons, the excellent acting of a part in

court and camp and council-room, and only when we try to
look into the heart of the man do we find that it is hardly
acting, after all, that the character has been converted
whole to the uses of this function, the individual utterly
eliminated, sublimated, if you will.   There is no Henry, only
a king.

I think Shakespeare was profoundly interested in this
particular study.   Not, indeed, by the character, for there is
no character, but by the singular circumstances of its dis-
appearance.   Neither we the readers nor Henry himself
nor his God ever meets the individual that had once under-
lain the outer crust that covers a Tudor monarch, for there
is nothing beneath the crust; all has been converted into
it; all desires, all impulses, all selfhood, all spirit.   He is
never alone, even with his God—least of all when he prays,
for then he is more than ever in the council chamber driving
an astute bargain, a piece of shrewd diplomacy, between one
king and another.

> O God of battles, steel my soldiers' hearts,
> Possess them not with fear.   Take from them now
> The sense of reckoning if th' opposed numbers
> Pluck their hearts from them.   Not to-day, O Lord,
> O, not to-day, think not upon the fault
> My father made, in compassing the crown.
> I Richard's body have interred new,
> And on it have bestowed more contrite tears,
> Than from it issued forced drops of blood.
> Five hundred poor I have in yearly pay.
> Who twice a day their wither'd hands hold up
> Toward Heaven, to pardon blood.   And I have built
> Two chantries, where the sad and solemn priests
> Sing still for Richard's soul.   More will I do,
> Though all that I can do is nothing worth;
> Since that my penitence comes after all,
> Imploring pardon.

This king, as Shakespeare portrays him, is indeed ' a
wondrous necessary man ', the keystone upon which the
sixteenth-century state depends, and individuality has at
last been subjugated wholly to the demands of office.   But
it is not for nothing that generations of Shakespeare's readers
have found little to love in this play.   Unless we read it in
the light of a certain bitter, underlying commentary, implicit
in the orientation of the chief character, there is little there

but that most grievous product of unremitting office, a dead man walking.

For the truth is that Shakespeare himself, now that he has built the figure with such care, out of the cumulative experience of eight plays, begins to recoil from it. It has been an experiment, an exploration, like, but for its larger scale, his brief but effective exploration of the system of Machiavelli, and, as he did with that system, so he does with this vast body of assembled evidence on public life : he rejects its findings as invalid before the deeper demands of the less explicit but immutable laws of man's spirit.

So much, then, for the Elizabethan phase of Shakespeare's portrait of the statesman-king, for the record of the period when he for a time believed that the wide canvas of public life was greater than the illimitable experience of the spirit. The contrast between the private and public virtues has been made clear, the qualifications of the great statesman have been slowly selected, tested, and built up into a single figure. Such characteristics as did not contribute to his public self have been eliminated (and they are seen, somewhat surprisingly, to be nearly co-terminous with character). More than this, certain of the loyalties, decencies, and ideals most prized in an individual are found to be incompatible with the public virtues. Henry, who rejected Falstaff in circumstances which cannot be forgiven, will also, in the moment of crisis, bargain with his God like a pedlar. His religion and his love for his people alike carry with them a tinge of expediency, a hint of the glib platform speaker.

It would seem, then, that in the very act of completing the figure, Shakespeare became aware of a certain insufficiency, and that dissatisfaction was already implicit in his treatment of Henry V, the culminating study of the series. What was there implicit is revealed by degrees in his treatment in the later plays of similar characters, or characters similarly placed. At the risk of straying a little from the immediate content of this discussion, may we consider Shakespeare's final comments ? For the additional significance they lend to the earlier figure makes it yet more comprehensive because of the latent subtlety, the implicit qualification that they bring to light in it.

Now, in the very play which concluded his Elizabethan picture, Shakespeare indicates already the tone and direction of his Jacobean commentary, which is at first merely dissatisfaction and disillusionment. In the course of the corollaries added in the Jacobean period it becomes clear that the disillusionment follows his perception of the true nature of Henry's supreme achievement, the whole and integral subordination of his individuality to the office of leadership. Shakespeare never again gives us a full picture of a successful ruler, with the exception of the figure of Claudius (the somewhat cynical implications of this selection constitute a study in themselves) and for the most part the men who fail, in the Jacobean plays, to meet the demands of public life are of interest not because they prove unfit for office, but because they are unfitted by office for something which Shakespeare increasingly perceives to be of deeper value.

Brutus is the first character in whom Shakespeare studied the wreckage that can be made of a man's conduct and career by the attempt to subject to the traffic of public life ideals deriving from values that cannot necessarily be carried into it. Brutus himself has an intuition of this when he pleads at the beginning with Cassius not to

> Have me seek into myself
> For that which is not in me.

For what is in him, the clear sense of justice, the deep honourableness, the assumption that all other men's actions rest on the same spring of honour and clear vision, serve not to better the state, but only to wreck it and him. A coarser and shrewder mind, having the sense to ' hold the world but as the world ', could have served the state more effectively. Cassius, from the first, acts openly ' in envy of great Cæsar ', but Brutus is blinded even to this by his preoccupation with ' the general good ', unaccompanied as it is by the essential knowledge of how the world lives. The illumination of his nobler conception cannot be expressed directly in action—not, certainly, by the man whose function it is to transmit the illumination—and this inference, if we are justified in making it of Brutus, points on to the conclusion finally reached in *Antony and Cleopatra*.

But whatever may happen to the conduct and career of the man who mistakenly offers himself to public service, the personality, in this first study, survives the wreck unspoiled. Cassius is wrong, as usual, when he assumed that Brutus's

> honourable metal may be wrought
> From that it is disposed.

The most he does is to make Brutus deceive himself as to the nature of his function, not as to the nature or truth of his vision. Brutus does, indeed, a certain violence to himself in setting before him a picture of an ideal Roman citizen and insisting that he can and must become that man, a theme that Shakespeare explores again and more searchingly in Coriolanus. But Brutus escapes the last penalties even of this; ' I slew my best lover for the good of Rome ', but he can in part redeem it, for he has, when it comes to the test, ' the same dagger for myself '. One other comment Shakespeare makes upon the relations of the private and public virtues, fast separating themselves in his mind, when he exposes, though in no way bitterly, the artificiality of this standard of public conduct. In Brutus's reception of the news of Portia's death—' Portia is dead. . . . Speak no more of her. . . . Well, to our work alive '—this becomes suddenly clear.[1] Ultimately Shakespeare was to overthrow the artificial and shallow conventions of conduct which public office, more than anything else, was likely to impose upon a man. In the meantime he is content to leave Brutus to reveal himself at death in the line ' I found no man but he was true to me ' (the personal relations filling his thought

---

[1] If further comment were needed, it is furnished by two still clearer episodes in the later play of *Macbeth*; one where Siward's stoical reception of his son's death is rebuked by Malcolm's natural humanity, another where Macduff makes his unanswerable appeal to genuine manhood against the artificial standard of conventional manliness :

> Dispute it like a man !
>   I shall do so.
> But I must also feel it as a man.

This, a far more assured and mature comment (not without interesting analogies in other contemporary dramatists), reflects back upon the conventional stoicism of the public man in Brutus and leaves us no doubt as to the conclusion Shakespeare had already drawn there.

at the last), and to conclude all upon the significant comment
' His life was gentle '.

After Brutus, the studies of the effect of public life upon
the mind are, for a time, either cynical or tragic. All are
studies of disaster in the soul, disaster which seems final in
the Duke of Vienna, Angelo, Macbeth, and Coriolanus, and
redeemed in Lear only by the miracle of suffering.

The companion studies in *Measure for Measure* stand
together; the Duke, who has brought to cunning perfection
Henry V's tactics in manipulating his people while adding to
them a stronger spice of Machiavelli's, and Angelo, whom he
chooses, with matchless irony, as an upright pillar of society.
Public life has taken its part in the subversion of both these
characters. They are not the only hypocrites in the play,
but their particular blends of deception and self-deception
are those that it peculiarly fosters. The deep and almost
irreparable division in the mind of Angelo comes of the
lifelong demeanour of a decent citizen unconsciously supported, like one of Ibsen's ' pillars of society ', by the picture
of himself that he finds in other men's eyes. The test of
contact with Isabella discovers to him a self far other, that
public life had hitherto allowed him to hide from. He
would be, were it not for his conversion by exposure, as clear
a case as could be found of the man

> Qui notus nimis omnibus
> Ignotus moritur sibi.

The two great tragic studies which contribute something
to our knowledge of Shakespeare's Jacobean comment on the
effects of office upon the individual fall into line rather with
the latest plays than with the earlier. In Macbeth and in
Lear the catastrophe goes deeper than with Brutus; nobility
of nature is poisoned or driven askew by power rather than
wrecked by the assumption of mistaken responsibilities.
Personality itself is touched, but by the privilege of leadership, not by its demands. Though the theme of *Macbeth*
is chiefly the Æschylean one of crime begetting crime, yet
the ' insolence of office ' has its share in the growth of that
megalomania which cries, ' For mine own good All causes
shall give way '. The companion study in *Lear* is that of a

man already formed, before the play opens, by the slower working of a more extended term of privilege. He, like an earlier king, was ' not born to sue but to command '; absorbed in the imperiousness that is the natural growth of unrestricted privilege, even in a magnanimous nature, he ' hath ever but slenderly known himself '. Had not catastrophe redeemed him, had it not been for the realization, ' I have ta'en too little care of this ', he too might have suffered the fate of Seneca's king : ' Ignotus moritur sibi.'

Indeed, it is this hiding of the self from the man who escapes it in public life that Shakespeare examines in the last of the great negative studies of the Jacobean series. Coriolanus is the companion figure in the later period, to Henry V in the Elizabethan. The distinction between the figures of Henry V and Coriolanus reveals the distance that Shakespeare's mind has travelled in the interval and the finality of his verdict on his own earlier creation. For Coriolanus is a study of a man bred and reared to public life from infancy, regardless of the suitability of his tempera- ment for the task. He has not, like Henry, subjugated himself to it deliberately ; he has been dedicated by Volumnia to the code of his caste. From this springs a mind more deeply divided even than Angelo's, and from that in turn the catastrophe that overwhelms him and nearly subverts the state. Because the identification of man and office has not been spontaneous, the individual that was Coriolanus has been not transmuted, but suppressed. The natural character has never been allowed to grow, and so it has become stunted, thwarted, and ill-regulated, as unreliable and unpredictable as the Roman mob, which is its image in the outward action of the play. More even than Lear or Leontes, he ' hath ever but slenderly known himself ', but unlike them he speaks a strange jargon of conventional Roman sentiment, appearing to think in terms of service and of loyalties utterly alien to the ruthless, self-seeking underlying nature. For Coriolanus, throughout his career, is acting. But as he has not identified himself with his part and become lost in it like Henry V, his sedulous training in public life never quite serves to restrain the hysterical outbursts of rebellion from the inner self that he has never met. He is perfect in the words and

gestures of a Roman noble; the generosity to his public
foe, Aufidius, the little touches of would-be magnanimity to
dependants, the blunt, honest soldier's refusal to take
rewards or hear his ' nothings monstered ', the deference to
Cominius and the senior men of his own party, to his mother
and to his wife (a deference which never, somehow, quite
amounts to considerateness)—all these he has at his command, and so long as the situations are those he has been
schooled to meet, he can present a tolerably coherent and
unified front to life. He can say, almost in the words of
Brutus, that

> brave death out-weighs bad life,
> And that his country's dearer than himself,

but the fine speeches, the schooled responses, the conditioned
reactions, all collapse when the unknown, underlying self is
touched by catastrophic failure. This life-long public self
stripped away, the maimed personality does not (as indeed
it cannot now) seek to discover itself, but only hurries, like
a dislodged hermit crab, to find another shell. The ruthless
training for office and public life has wrought its full and fatal
effect.

As in the preliminary or minor histories Shakespeare gave
a mainly negative conclusion on the nature of kingship and
followed it up in the major histories by a positive study of
what kingship was, so, in the Jacobean plays, he gives first
a series of studies (though far less definitely orientated or
closely correlated) of individuals sacrificed in one way or
another to the exigencies of public life, and leads up to a final
and positive study of the individual spirit triumphing over
the less substantial claims, the more superficial values of the
other. The last detailed comment is that of *Antony and
Cleopatra*, which is like a symphonic rendering of the passionate theme of individual freedom, not the childish egotism of
Henry VI or Richard II or that later modification in Lear
and Macbeth, but the mature realization that upon the
individual life of the spirit the world of affairs could have no
final claim.

The whole course, then, of Shakespeare's survey of this
problem, the choosing out by trial and error of the qualifications proper to a great statesman-king, the welding together

of these findings into a single figure, the subsequent surveying
of this figure and its implications from a distance and from
a world of experience quite other, and the ultimate abandon-
ment both of the figure and of the claims it represented, the
whole course of this survey resolves itself ultimately into one
conclusion, harmonious alike with the main body of Shakespeare's thought and with the conclusions reached simultaneously by the finest poetic thought of his contemporaries.   It
is a magnificent plea, first negative and then positive, for the
supreme claims of the individual spirit.   Shakespeare, from
the first, sees, as clearly as Chapman, that there was little
place for it in public life, that public life was not best served
by it, but he sees equally clearly, and he sees it at the last,
that neither is this spirit itself best served by public life.
For Shakespeare, the second conclusion, the final pronounce-
ment of his experience upon this theme, is the valid one.

Of his view of conduct as itself a supreme art, Shakespeare
surrenders nothing in this latest phase; but the quality of
the conduct which interests him changes profoundly.   He, no
less than Ford or Webster, sees in it the possibility of
sublimity, but, like them, and indeed like all the Jacobeans,
he no longer finds its essential expression in the council
chamber, the battlefield or the forum, but rather in the inner
recesses of the spirit, revealed, if revealed at all, by chance
or the accident of affinity.   He must have recognized the
echo of his own thought in Webster's words,

> For know, whether I am doomed to live or die
> I can do both like a prince,

the words in which his duchess declares her allegiance not to a
pattern of conduct imposed by social demands, but to an
inner aristocratic ideal, unrealized even by the character
itself until that moment.   For Shakespeare, too, had by
then explored those minds whose purpose is not so much the
presentation of a certain figure to the world as obedience to
the guidance of certain perceptions, perceptions that not only
cannot be directly expressed in public life, but may even be
contaminated in the attempt at such direct expression.
Henry V and Coriolanus are concerned to present a design
for living whose main lines they themselves (with varying

completeness) already know. But Hamlet, Lear, Timon, Cleopatra, Antony are concerned not at all with presenting a figure of such and such design, and hardly at all with that conscious uttering of principle in word and action that makes up public conduct. They proceed instead by a half-unconscious subordination of action, and even thought, to the guidance of some often undefined principle (itself perhaps at variance with the verdict of the world or unapprehended by it), which transmutes the character into something of which it itself would remain incompletely aware, unless released in a moment of tragic crisis.

That citadel of absolute truth, the inner self hardly known to the man himself, may be corrupted by the effort to stage himself to the public eye, and to surrender to the demand of public life may well be fatal to that core of the spirit wherein is stored its potential immortality.

Shakespeare's final position is an uncompromising declaration of individual freedom and responsibility, that supreme virtue of which the Jacobeans knew so well the value. ' I have in this rough work shaped out a man.' He has, indeed, throughout the Jacobean period : Brutus, Hamlet, Macbeth, Lear, Timon, Antony, Cleopatra, Prospero. And the shaping has involved the rejection not of Falstaff, but of Henry V.

It is the shaping out of this ' man ', the creation of this figure which is no one man but an image to which many characters bring their parts, that makes the historical and political group organic.[1] To maintain that the political plays, even the four that make up the central group, are equivalent to an epic would be a piece of foolish extremism.

[1] It may be urged that these plays are not a planned sequence, that there can therefore have been no continuous design (as in the *Oresteia*) and that the whole cannot have cohered in Shakespeare's mind as the living parts of a great work of art cohere to make an organic whole. In support of this it might be pointed out that the plays were written at fairly wide intervals. But the vast organism of a major work of art must always be held in the artist's mind through a considerable period of time, even if it finally takes the form of a single poem. Interruption of work upon it, the suspension of attention for a time, need not destroy the fundamental continuity of thought or the organic nature of the work of art that is finally produced. How long did Milton hold *Paradise Lost* in mind ? And how long did Goethe hold *Faust* ?

A work of art cannot at the same time be two different works of art. But it is possible to consider that the sequence, through the continuous presence of this image of the statesman-king, is able to subdue to the dramatic form the vast and apparently undramatic matter of potential epic, without losing the peculiar virtue of epic material, coherent presentation of spaciousness, and of the multifariousness of life.

In Shakespeare's history plays we have, then, I believe, a second instance of hard-won reconciliation of seemingly alien content with dramatic form.

CHAPTER FOUR

'DISCORD IN THE SPHERES': THE UNI-VERSE OF *TROILUS AND CRESSIDA*

THE great play of *Troilus and Cressida*, one of the most weighty in the Jacobean period, has had a strange fate. Its readers have been variously affected by it, and our reflections, when we have not taken refuge in silence, have ranged from dismissing it as a piece of hasty work to defending it as a failure on a grand scale. Commentators [1] describe, in the one case, the ill-digested scenes mixed with graver, sometimes noble, matter, and in the other point out that, though Shakespeare had undoubtedly something which he wished to say (and to say in specifically dramatic terms), he for once mistook ' what may be digested in a play ', and, by sheer pressure of content, broke the mould he tried to use.

By repeated readings of the play, helped greatly by seeing it upon the stage, by trying to relate it to the criticism of life offered by some of Shakespeare's Jacobean contemporaries (to say nothing of the criticism of life implicit in some of our own contemporaries), I am driven to believe that this is not enough; that the play of *Troilus and Cressida* is not a great failure to record a phase of experience beyond the scope of dramatic form, but a great achievement, perhaps one of the greatest, in the expression of that phase, transcending those limitations to produce a living work of art.[2] That the actual experience which is thus expressed is of deep significance to our generation I no more doubt than

[1] These, ranging from Coleridge in the early nineteenth century to Professor F. S. Boas in our own time, with the addition of the quite recent work of Professor Wilson Knight and W. W. Lawrence, however widely they differ otherwise, agree in remarking in some way upon the contradictions in mood and assessments of values to be found in the play.
[2] I was for many years satisfied to see in this play a momentary failure of Shakespeare's artistic power. The failure was, on the contrary, in my understanding. It would be well, no doubt, if every critic were to hang upon the wall of his workroom the timely admonition : ' 'Tis not Homer nods but we that sleep.'

that it is essential to our understanding of Shakespeare's later tragic and constructive plays; but for the generations between Shakespeare's and our own it has been generally avoidable, and therefore rare. It is no light matter to suggest that something in any way important to our understanding of the play should have escaped a long succession of commentators. Nor would anyone venture upon doing so today, were it not that our actual experience of disintegration and disruption, so unlike that of any age between, has thrown fresh light upon the nature and foundations of what we call civilization; prospects once mercifully rare are now common and familiar, and much that has not, in the interval, been generally forced upon the imagination, now lies upon the common road for every man's necessary consideration.

The great plays that follow this one in psychological sequence,[1] *Timon of Athens* and *King Lear*, are expressions of a further phase of the same experience; disintegration is accomplished, ' Nature's germens tumble all together, Even till destruction sicken ' and the judgement surrenders. In the moment of surrender the mind perceives another dimension of reality, and this perception leads in the end to the positive, spiritual revaluation in the last plays. But *Troilus and Cressida* stands at a lower point of negation in this sequence than *Lear* or even *Timon*. For, while its material is still that of the actual world, the mood is that of a man who has come to the end of that world's resources; emotional, intellectual, and moral values resolve alike into futility;

[1] It is the psychological sequence rather than the chronological that mainly concerns us here. It is undoubtedly possible for a mature artist to produce works in an order which does not precisely represent the order of the phases through which his mind is progressing at that time. This is made clear in the cases of some later artists who have left, in letters and journals, a complementary record of their thought and experience. The letters of Ibsen, taken in conjunction with his plays, are, of course, one of the most familiar examples of this kind of record, showing this kind of variation, in modern dramatic art. With the Jacobean playwrights many factors, even including professional demands, would be at work, but more important than these would still be those revivals and recrudescences of earlier moods which often characterize the apparent irregularities of spiritual growth. It is for this reason that we may discover some of the relations between Shakespeare's plays more clearly by considering them in what we believe to be their psychological sequence rather than in what we conjecture to be their chronological.

E

even the imagination, the high constructive power, looking
ahead into a dark night of the soul, sees no further ideal
form, no ' unbodied figure of the thought ' waiting upon
creation.   This last experience is an area of suffering peculiar
to the artist's mind, but it can derive from an experience
potentially common to all men, the vision of the disjunction
and disintegration of civilization—the ideals it rests upon
and the achievements it bequeaths—while these are still
co-extensive for him with the universe of thought.   It is, in
fact, in this very image that Shakespeare chooses to embody
his experience in this play.   What is recorded in *Troilus and
Cressida* is thus the acutest point of suffering in this sequence,
before the understanding has surrendered its moral, intellectual, or imaginative synthesis and accepted disintegration;
the fullest possible realization of imminent dissolution
before its accomplishment brings anæsthesia.

Readers of drama often receive piecemeal the experience
of which a play is the record, looking first at individual parts
or aspects of it; indeed, it requires either the highest imaginative capacity or prolonged knowledge to receive so complex
and so vast an artistic experience as is communicated by a
great play.   Let us concede to this habit for the moment, if
only because it will take us by the shortest road to some
essential truths about *Troilus and Cressida*, the consideration
of various single aspects being a kind of preliminary exercise
before we attempt to receive the communication of the
artistic experience.

In *Troilus and Cressida* the aspect we are first aware of is,
as in many plays, the material of which it is made.   For the
artist this has meant the choosing, from the infinite and
unselected mass of life, of those groups of characters and
events to which his mind turns for the purposes of its as yet
undefined interpretation; it is the first step in the substitution of the form of art for the chaos of life.   For the reader
it means the subject-matter of the play and his general
impression derived from it; the series of characters, the
chronological sequence of events, the impinging of character
and event upon each other.   And in *Troilus and Cressida*
this takes the form of a succession of violently contrasted
characters, events, and sentiments.   Characters as dis-

cordant as Thersites and Troilus, Nestor and Pandarus, Hector and Cressida, Agamemnon and Achilles are forced into continual and jarring contrast, with no attempt to resolve the contradictions in an enveloping mood of humour or pity. Instead, the nucleus of the character-grouping, upon which our attention is continually focussed as in a well-composed picture, is that of Troilus and Cressida; a serious man, by nature heroic and an honest if confused idealist, and a light woman, equally by nature a

> sluttish spoil of opportunity
> And daughter of the game.

The same pitiless enforcing of contrasts is seen in the relation of character and event, the incompatibility of men's endeavours and their destinies; the ideal love of Troilus and the betrayal it meets at the height of its glory; the honourable, heroic code of Aeneas and Diomede, Hector and Agamemnon, and the collapse of that code in Achilles' murder of Hector; the clear, sustained thought of the debates upon principles and policy in the Greek and Trojan council chambers, and the relapse into petty feuds and ambushes, which serves to show how far that noble sanity can work upon event. And as we watch these passions, ideas, and achievements annihilate each other with no promise of compensation or solution, we fall more and more into agreement with Thersites, the showman who is ever at hand to point the futility, the progressive cancelling out to negation.

The materials of *Troilus and Cressida* are thus more obviously at war than those of any other play of Shakespeare's, and their discord has been a main factor in persuading its readers of the unevenness of the play, of the inconsistency in quality and treatment of the different parts, attributable, it might be, to indifference or weariness in the writer or to alternating and unreconciled moods of admiration on the one hand and expostulation, disgust, or disillusionment upon the other.

But what if this effect be itself art? What if disharmony be, not the result of a photographic reproduction of materials that the artist's mind has registered without full comprehension, but a deliberate commentary? For, significant and familiar as is the bitterness, the loathing of life which brought together the elements of *Troilus and Cressida*, the apposing of these is even more notable than the choosing. That aspect of a play which its readers think of as its form is itself a mode of interpretation of the material, having been for the artist the next step in the freeing of ' that unbodied figure of the thought, That gave it surmised shape '. The elements fall into such positions or relations within the scheme of his play as not only emphasize and disengage the nature and quality of each, but indicate the underlying values by which his interpretation of the material was determined.

This is revealed first and most obviously in the sequence of the scenes, and here the effect is best appreciated in a rapid production which preserves the Elizabethan tempo and forces us to see one scene running as it were into the next; by insisting upon their almost merging in presentation, it makes clear to us that they must be merged also in our interpretation; that they are, in fact, inseparable. Thersites or Pandarus (the explicit or the implicit statement of the mood of disillusionment) breaks in upon every scene in which nobility of conception, passion, or conduct is emphasized, following it up, almost before the echoes of the last words have died away. The induction and the conclusion are in the hands of Pandarus. Pandarus' talk precedes the great council-chamber scene in the Greek camp, where Ulysses builds his lofty image of the state; and Nestor and Ulysses (two of the wisest figures of the play) are hardly off the stage before the scurrilous venom of Thersites is poured upon them in the next scene. Straight upon this comes the corresponding council debate in Troy, with its penetrating analysis of one of the fundamentals of the play, the nature of value; and straight upon that again, Thersites calling up vengeance, ' or, rather, the Neapolitan bone-ache ', upon both armies. Into this meeting of Thersites and Patroclus come again the Greek leaders, their lofty statesmanship tinged now perforce with politic cunning, and upon that again the scene (III, i) between Pandarus, Paris, and Helen; the feverish frivolity of the background of the war jars bitterly with the scenes of camp and battle and yet is inextricably interwoven with

them.   Straight upon their urbane and matter-of-fact jesting
upon the habit of love, come Troilus's ideal, tremulous
anticipations, and into this very scene again, Pandarus, that
' wondrous necessary man '.   This handling continues all
through the play, but the sifting together of the elements
becomes closer and closer as it goes on; Pandarus is nearly
always present with Troilus and Cressida in Troy, and
Thersites takes his place in the scene of Troilus's disillusionment in the Greek camp.   The highest altitudes of chivalry
are touched in the scene of Hector's visit to Agamemnon,
where a noble code makes possible this courteous friendship
between honourable enemies.   The scene is set between that
which sees Cressida ' wide unclasp the table of her thoughts
To every ticklish reader ' and that in which Thersites de-
nounces Patroclus's relations with Achilles.   This does not
seem like accident.

There is something, then, in the form of this play which
leads us to believe in its unity of intention.   Moreover, the
belief that it is not inconsequent and contradictory but
intent and purposeful, is confirmed by our first experience
of the imagery and the prosody.   The tough resilience of the
verbal music, the explosive illumination of the imagery are
the marks of a causal, not a casual, direction.   The speeches
of Ulysses, Agamemnon, Hector, and Nestor are distinguished
by close-woven, intricate, and virile imagery, and the ring
of the verse throughout these scenes is superb.   When
Ulysses persuades the Greek councillors, he gives a noble
smoothness and simplicity of line to his doctrine of hierarchical ' degree '.   When Nestor is alone with Ulysses, a
mind thewed like his own, he speaks with cryptic cogency a
language of brief hints weighted with implications that he
need not elucidate, so that, by the interlocking of imagery,
the work of argument itself is done by the images.[1]   In
neither of these quite different uses of imagery and musical
units is there any suggestion of faltering power or purpose :

> Yet in the trial much opinion dwells.
> For here the Trojans taste our dear'st repute
> With their fin'st palate.   And trust to me, *Ulysses,*
> Our imputation shall be oddly pois'd

---

[1] See Chapter V, ' The Functions of Imagery in Drama '.

> In this wild action. For the success
> (Although particular) shall give a scantling
> Of good or bad unto the general.
> And in such indexes, although small pricks
> To their subsequent volumes, there is seen
> The baby figure of the giant mass
> Of things to come at large. It is suppos'd
> He that meets Hector issues from our choice;
> And choice, being mutual act of all our souls,
> Makes merit her election, and doth boil,
> As 'twere from forth us all, a man distill'd
> Out of our virtues; who miscarrying,
> What heart receives from hence the conquering part,
> To steel a strong opinion to themselves?
> Which entertain'd limbs are his instruments,
> In no less working than are swords and bows
> Directive by the limbs.

It is this virility, the basis of the style, running beneath the froth and fantasy of the Pandarus–Helen scenes, emerging suddenly in a different tempo in Thersites' ecstasies of abuse, which binds the whole together, showing one mind at work, and that an undivided mind, beneath the seeming variations. Moreover, the apposition (in such a speech as this of Nestor) of images that, while leading in the reader's mind to a process equivalent to arguing, do indeed fly off from each other ' with impetuous recoile and jarring sound ', plays its own part in furthering that impression of disjunction which the art of the play, in major or in minor form, is ceaselessly at work to enforce upon us. The persistence, in fact, of such verse and imagery, right through to Troilus's last speech on the death of Hector, indicates, in a very different way but no less surely than the ruthless choice and the sure handling of material, that this is no plaything for Shakespeare. Here is a task upon which his whole mind was bent in intense and terrific concentration. Metre and imagery alike wrestle with their subject-matter. Every faculty works at its full height; the last resources of intellect and imagination are in action.

The conclusion, then, from even this brief consideration of the subject and form of the play, is that they collaborate, not fortuitously, but intentionally, that the form illuminates and interprets the theme, is itself ordered by it, each being in some degree an aspect of the other, precisely as we expect in a play which is a major work of dramatic art. And so

there is confirmed the impression that here is no failure,
nor even partial success. For, given discord as the central
theme, it is hard to imagine how else it should be formally
reflected but in a deliberately intended discord of form also.
Rare this may be—perhaps unique in dramatic art—but, as I
have suggested, the experience which the play exists to communicate is rare also. As readers, we, in effect, testify, by
the conviction that our impression has been conveyed by the
whole, and nothing less than the whole play, that the work of
art we are contemplating is a living organism, a single form
of perceived reality, however vast, complex, or difficult of
communication it may be.

With this conviction in mind, then, we can turn to the
underlying ideas of the play, no longer expecting to find
inconsistency in Shakespeare's treatment of the various parts.

It cannot escape our notice that, in *Troilus and Cressida*,
the revelation of the writer's values [1] is not, as in most of
Shakespeare's work, implicit only, and so dependent upon
our ability to receive the artistic experience of the dramatist[2];
there is also much explicit discussion of the abstract question,
' What is value? ' This is both easier to distinguish and a
direct road to Shakespeare's implicit comment, and for both
reasons it is well to consider it first.

Many of the characters—Troilus, Paris, Achilles, Hector,
Ulysses, Thersites—are either involved in a bitter fight to
harmonize the conflicting evidence of their universe, or are
gradually relaxing their efforts and subsiding into a no less
bitter equilibrium of disillusionment or loathing. As they

[1] There is some difficulty in finding a term for this. Were the
results of Shakespeare's implications positive, the term ' values ' would
be satisfactory. But the modern connotation is, rather, the categories
under which a man apprehends the good (see, for example, Inge,
Philosophy of Plotinus, Vol. II, pp. 74 *seq.*), and, since Shakespeare's
conclusion is negative, there is an undesirable element of paradox in
applying it here. The position is complicated by the fact that, while
his absolutes become evil, he has reached his conclusion by a process of
eliminating values. We should perhaps be technically accurate if we
said that his metaphysical ultimate is evil manifested in the form of
chaos—a negative form perhaps of Nietsche's ' Umwertung aller
Werte '.

[2] I think that it is still mainly so in *Troilus and Cressida*, and that it
is our doubt or inability at this point that has led to the misinterpreta-
tion of some of the values indicated in the play.

make their different interpretations of the meaning or non-meaning of that universe, it begins to be clear that many of the main issues depend for them upon the question of whether value is absolute or relative; inherent in the object or super-imposed upon it; objective or subjective to the valuer.

Troilus, at the beginning of the play, represents one extreme; he believes that the object of faith or worship (a woman, an ideal, a code, an institution) is invested with value precisely to the degree to which it is valued. ' What is aught ', he exclaims, ' but as 'tis valued ', and though it never occurs to him to consider the relation of this belief to his estimate of Cressida, there are signs of underlying misgiving in his constant questioning of her. The course of the play brings him out of his belief, through a process of disintegration in which the operation of reasoning is set against the faculty itself,[1] to a state of equilibrium in which he repudiates the two great ideals of his life, love and soldier-ship, betrayed in the one by Cressida's perfidy, in the other by the murder of Hector. In their romantic defence of the war at the beginning, he and Paris behave like book collectors who pay £100 for a rare example containing certain typo-graphical peculiarities, not because of its intrinsic beauty or interest, but because that market price has been fixed by other men's willingness to rise to it. For all its romantic dressing, this is at bottom the most purely commercial aspect of value presented in the play, equating merit with the price that can be got for a thing, Helen with so much warfare. When this is advanced in its turn as a reason for continuing to value her, it involves a bland *petitio principii* that neither of the hot-headed young men has time to observe :

> *Paris.* There's not the meanest spirit on our party
> Without a heart to dare, or sword to draw,
> When Helen is defended. . . . Then (I say)
> Well may we fight for her, whom we know well
> The world's large spaces cannot parallel.

If the fallacy of their arguments escapes their own notice, it does not escape that of Hector, the clearest exponent of

---

[1] See *Troilus and Cressida*, V, ii, 139–43.

the other view of value, value as something that must be
primarily inherent in the object valued :

> But value dwells not in particular will;
> It holds his estimate and dignity
> As well wherein 'tis precious of itself,
> As in the prizer : 'Tis mad idolatry
> To make the service greater than the God;
> And the will dotes that is inclinable
> To what infectiously itself affects,
> Without some image of th' affected merit.

It is, as he implies later, for lack of this ' image of the affected
merit ' that the arguments of Paris and Troilus are ' glozed
but superficially ' and are indeed no reasons.　He dismisses
the strongest argument on their side, namely that its effect
on its worshipper itself invests the idol with value (indeed,
with all the value we need to seek), temperately making it
clear that the sense of value depends for its stability upon
something outside itself, objective and absolute, inherent
in the object—in short, upon the ' image of the affected
merit '.

But many other characters in the play are seeking, by
different methods and with different incidental experience,
for just such an ' image '—an absolute value by which to test
the evidence of their experience.　And they all either come
to the same destructive conclusion or themselves furnish
notable confirmation by their fates of the destructive phil-
osophies of the rest.

Achilles, lazy in mind and body, is, when roused, no more
defective in intelligence than he is in professional skill.　The
sting of Agamemnon's insults drives him to some effortless
and quite lucid self-examination on the nature of reputation
and, as he falls in with Ulysses at the peak of his exasperation,
the discussion slides naturally into the major question of the
play, ' Is there or is there not in anything an absolute value ? '
Achilles makes for himself the discovery that reputation
(which he, being of the school of Troilus and Paris, equates
with value) determines a man's own view of himself.　Ulysses
clinches it for him : a man ' feels not what he owes [= owns],
but by reflection ', but he carries the investigation a step
further, and sees in reputation (the value other men put
upon a man) the necessary completion of a process without

which a quality does not fully exist. He equates it with the
function of communication as we understand it in art or in
love, without some form of which the process has not been
consummated. Indeed, Shakespeare lets him use that very
term :

> No man is the lord of any thing,
> (Though in and of him there is much consisting)
> Till he communicate his parts to others :
> Nor doth he of himself know them for ought,
> Till he behold them formed in th' applause,
> Where they are extended.

The essential relation between ' communication ' and
' form ' here is highly significant, as is the distinction between
Ulysses' position and that of Troilus, Paris, and Achilles.
Ulysses, who could speak later of the ' mystery, wherein
relation Durst never meddle, in the soul of state ', does not
deny the possibility of the absolute value that Hector insists
on. He merely points out the inseparable relationship
between the two aspects, intrinsic value and assessed value,
in man's experience, and declares that without the second
the first is unfulfilled. ' Else a great prince in prison lies.'

When we remember how unusual are discussions of
abstract themes in Shakespeare's plays as compared, for
instance, with Chapman's, Tourneur's, and Beaumont and
Fletcher's among his contemporaries, we may well pause to
ask what it means in *Troilus and Cressida*. In all the plays
in which something similar occurs (and never, not even in
Measure for Measure, is it so full and so penetrating) it is
also strictly integral to the main matter and so inwoven
with the action as to be a natural commentary upon it.
This is no less true of the discussions on the nature of kingship
and government in the sequence of history plays, especially
the two parts of *Henry IV* and *Henry V*, than of the reflections on the art of conduct in *Hamlet*. Arguing from this,
we may wonder whether this continual talk of values, this
debating to and fro not only of their nature, but of the
question of their existence, is not equally essential in some
way to the fundamental theme of *Troilus and Cressida*,
whether, in short, Shakespeare ever suffered his characters
to be deeply concerned with a question which was not the

core of the play. Is Shakespeare, in *Troilus and Cressida*, himself revealing, through their conscious analyses as through their experience, a state in which such questions met just such answers in his own mind? I think he is, and I think this brings us to the root of the matter. The writer of this play is a man to whom values have become suspect.

Were the wisdom of Hector and Ulysses allowed to survive, in contrast with the rest of the play but without further comment, this might be less clearly implied. But actually it suffers defeat in both cases; in Hector's by the implications of his betrayal at the hands of a code in whose stability he had trusted; in Ulysses', first by the course of the action, which denies the truth of his idea by the contradiction of event, and, secondly and more specifically, by a later admission of his own, when, arguing that virtue must not seek ' remuneration for the thing it is ', he goes on to dismiss the possibility of intrinsic value having, in practice and in the affairs of men, any effective alliance with assessed value :

> Love, friendship, charity, are subjects all
> To envious and calumniating time :

so that the indispensable condition, without which intrinsic value cannot be liberated into reality, is never there. The reason for this is at once simple and irremediable, it lies in the nature of man's mind :

> One touch of nature makes the whole world kin :
> That all with one consent praise new born gauds,
> Though they are made and moulded of things past,
> And give to dust, that is a little gilt,
> More laud than gilt o'er-dusted.

That is, man's judgement (his capacity for valuing) is incapable of its task, and absolute value, whether or not it exists, is never discernible.

Even the acute intelligence of Ulysses then, having done its best upon the problem, has met with implicit and explicit defeat, and it is not surprising that the same fate befalls the other characters.

The last position, in descending order of negation, is that of Thersites. He has long taken for granted the conclusion that Ulysses has implied; mankind in his eyes is as incapable of worthy judgement as of worthy conduct; Ulysses,

Nestor, Agamemnon, Hector and Troilus are reduced to
their lowest terms, no less than Achilles, Ajax, Patroclus,
Paris, Helen and Cressida. But he has travelled further.
He does not waste time debating the existence of absolute
value, or whether or not man can perceive and live by it;
he assumes no criterion beyond that fallible human judgement of which he is so eloquent a satirist. Nor does the
obscene casualty of fate and circumstance stagger him; for
here the paradoxes of circumstances have long ago taken the
wind of satire : ' To what form but that he is, should wit
larded with malice, and malice forced with wit turn him to ?
To an ass were nothing; he is both ass and ox; to an ox,
were nothing; he is both ox and ass.' In the world he
offers us there is no stability in character, ideals, institutions,
judgement, nor in imagination itself. The whole is a shifting,
heaving morass where all is relative and nothing absolute,
where pullulating worm and insect forms, seething upon the
surface, are seen suddenly, as at the dissipating of some soft,
concealing cloud, intent upon their task of disintegration and
erosion, reducing all things to their own terms and substance.

And yet Thersites is an integral part of the play's form
and matter, and that play is a living organism. It is upon
the whole fabric that his mind is at work, driven by the passion of his disgust to break down the forms of things into
lifeless elements that can never again be human flesh and
blood nor even wholesome earth, but must remain barren
and negative like deflowered soil. As we read his comment
and relate it with the debates in these other minds, his is
seen to be the dominant of their scale. For he, to whom
all the argument is a cuckold and a whore, who sees the
common curse of mankind, folly and ignorance, as deserving
only the dry serpigo and war and lechery to confound them,
has arrived at his conclusion by the very road that they are
travelling—Ulysses by his own reasoning, Troilus by the
conversion wrought in him by event, and the rest by their
betrayal of or at the hands of their codes. The starting-
point of his interpretation is the conclusion to which they
too are proceeding : there is no absolute value inherent in
the universe imaged in the loves and wars of Greeks and
Trojans. There *is* no ' image of the affected merit '.

Once we have isolated this central question (What is the nature of value and has it or has it not an absolute existence ?), once we have traced the series of positions, from positive to negative, of Hector, Troilus, Ulysses, and Thersites and the relation of each of those positions to the general evidence of the play, matter and form alike are seen to derive from this conclusion, which makes of the whole a vast, complex but organic artistic experience. The conflict between conduct, ideals, and event which the choice of material lays so clearly before us and the idea of disjunction inescapably enforced by the structure of the play serve now to drive home the conclusion that in this play disjunction was a fundamental principle, if not the most fundamental, in Shakespeare's view of the universe of event.

But we are uneasily aware, at the same time, that this judgement is not limited to the universe of event. Were that so, we should probably find in this play a mood of partial negation only, as in the balanced conflicts of the tragedies, where the positive element contends on equal terms with the negative and the duality is essential in the artistic experience. But in *Troilus and Cressida* our sense of the artistic unity has derived, as we have realized, not from an impression of balance, but from an impression of evil enveloping apparent good; not from a picture of the accidental prevalence of mischance and injustice over wisdom and rectitude, but from the implication of a causal relation between disjunction in event and the absence of absolute criteria in the universe of thought. To make this clear we may look again at some of the noblest thought in the play and see how it is related to the enveloping and prevailing evil and how its destruction carries the principle of disjunction into the domain of the mind itself.

Let us take again Ulysses' defence of ' degree ', the foundation upon which civilization and its achievement rests. The hierarchy of his state stands, in its nobility of conception, linked with the hierarchy of the heavens, a microcosm of the great universe :

> The Heavens themselves, the planets, and this centre,
> Observe degree, priority, and place,

and ' all in line of order '. The heavens maintain their

courses and the world of man reflects their ordered process
in ' The unity and married calm of states '. But if the
planets ' in evil mixture to disorder wander ', then ' Degree
is shak'd ', both in the cosmos and in society, the image of
the cosmos created by man's mind. Then, in the two
universes alike, in that of the material cosmos and that of
man's creating ' each thing meets in mere oppugnancy ', and
chaos is come again. To this ' mere oppugnancy ' the play
leads us inescapably, by the matter and texture of the concluding acts. The towering thoughts and ideals topple down
before a destiny as implacable as that foreseen by Ulysses
for the doomed towers of Troy; and if we look immediately
from these ideals to the last phases of the action, the ambush
and murder of Hector, we have no choice but to measure
the chaos and the discord by the gracious assurance, the
magnanimity, and the seeming stability that they destroy.
Just as we feel the value of the *Oedipus* or the *Oresteia* to
be in one way commensurate with the depth and the power
of evil which Sophocles and Aeschylus meet and transmute,
so in *Troilus* the nobility of that order which in the end
proves perishable gives us the measure of the destructive
forces which triumph over it. The existence of the principle
of cause and order (in the cosmos and in the affairs of men) is
therein questioned; it vanishes, revealing destruction as the
principle underlying all life.

The supreme reach, moreover, of Shakespeare's imagery
and prosody in this play, with all that they imply of sustained
imaginative thought, serve also by their association with
the prevailing evil, to affirm the magnitude and universality
of that evil when it does prevail :

> But the strong base and building of my love
> Is as the very centre of the earth,
> Drawing all things to it.

It is Cressida speaking; and when the base of the world,
the centre of stability itself, is equated with Cressida's love,
we have not much farther to seek for Shakespeare's comment
upon that stability.

Moreover, the downfall of the principles of order and value
in the world of man's creation, with the substitution of the

negative principles of disjunction and chaos, is traced directly
to that inability in man to imagine absolute value which we
have already recognized; in Ulysses's words, to the ' touch
of nature ' that ' makes the whole world kin '. It *is*, indeed,
man's ' nature '. Not only is the objective universe, then,
the cosmos and society, found subject to this curse of disjunction; the universe of the imagination also is proved
incapable of conceiving a stable value. Disjunction, chaos,
discord in the spheres, this is the only irreducible and continuing thing. The denial of absolute value, of any real
' image of the affected merit ', is, then, carried beyond the
world of event within the play; casualty has replaced
causality in the world of the imagination also.

It would seem, then, that this play is an attempt, upon a
scale whose vastness is measured by the intensity with which
every faculty of the poet's mind is engaged, to find that
image (of absolute value) in the evidence of man's achievement, in the sum or parts of his experience or, if nowhere
else, in the processes of creative imagination. Troilus's love,
Agamemnon's chivalry, Ulysses's vision of the hierarchy of
state are all, thus, experimental images, in which are tested
the absolute value of man's passion, intellect, and imagination. In face of this test, this ' Quid hoc ad æternitatem ? ',
all fail. There is no absolute quality the evidence for which
does not resolve itself into a mere subjective illusion of blood
or fancy, a

> mad idolatry,
> To make the service greater than the God.

The creations of man's spirit, hitherto exalted, are now seen
to have survived only by chance, at the mercy all the time
of a stronger, natural law of destruction; what in another
mood might have appeared tragic accidents, the counter-
point in a fuller harmony, are now seen, instead, to reveal
an underlying law to which all is recurrently and inescapably
subject. This is the ultimate, indeed the only surviving
absolute in *Troilus and Cressida*. The faculty that could
perceive degree and the ordered form of a universe, the
imagination itself, has been touched and the images of form
no longer rise at its command. ' There is no more to say.'
The dark night of the soul comes down upon the unillumin-

ated wreckage of the universe of vision.   The play of *Troilus
and Cressida* remains as one of the few living and unified
expressions of this experience.

The grand scale of this catastrophe blinds us.   We do not
willingly imagine this overthrow; some at least of us never
to the end comprehend it, for it is like a note too deep for
our hearing, or a landscape too vast for our experiencing.
We probably come nearer to understanding the tragedies
than this play which is no tragedy and is yet perhaps the
record of the profoundest catastrophe in man's experience.

> Moving of th' earth brings harms and fears,
>   Men reckon what it did and meant,
> But trepidation of the spheres,
>   Though greater far, is innocent.

If we turn from this attempt to understand the nature of
the underlying ideas in *Troilus and Cressida* and consider the
form through which these ideas are revealed, we see that
what has been achieved is in fact what we suggested at the
outset.   The idea of chaos, of disjunction, of ultimate formlessness and negation, has by a supreme act of artistic mastery
been given form.   It has not been described in more or less
abstract terms; it has been imaged.   What seemed to be
an absolute limitation of drama has been transcended and
shown, in this rare achievement, to be but relative.

And in this case, even more than in either of those which
we have just considered, the subduing of content to form is
no mere act of virtuosity; it has a further significance as an
instance of one of the ultimate functions of art.

That the experience on which this play rests is of profound
significance at any time, and of peculiar significance to our
own, needs no discussion.   Whenever actual experience
threatens to pass endurance, there is a measure of alleviation in discovering that it has already been met and
recorded.   The facts are not softened, but the sense of
isolation which gives the facts a main part of their horror is
mitigated; the desert is no less to be reckoned with, but
something is gone if it is no longer ' terra incognita ' nor
utterly unmapped.   When we find, as we certainly do in this
play, not merely a record of actual experience, but a communication of an artistic experience, the alleviation becomes

more positive; the actual experience, in that case, has not only been met, but resolved into form by the grandest of all human faculties, the artistic imagination. Once it has been encompassed by this imagination, at whatever cost, the bounds of human comprehension have been set forward in proportion as it had appeared incomprehensible. The value that we finally attach in this way, to Aeschylus, to Sophocles, and to Shakespeare rests upon the extent of their comprehension of evil, and upon the extent to which that vision of evil has been brought under the governance of those artistic laws which are themselves the image of the ultimate law of an ordered universe. Thus, in Shakespeare's *Troilus and Cressida* we meet a paradoxical dualism. The content of his thought is an implacable assertion of chaos as the ultimate fact of being; the presence of artistic form is a deeper, unconscious testimony to an order which is actually ultimate and against which the gates of hell shall not prevail.

This is made clearer still by the direction his thought takes in the plays that follow *Troilus and Cressida* and lead on in direct succession to the final group. This subduing of matter to form in the earlier play is then seen to be prophetic of a resolution not only of the technical problem of relating content to form, but of the dualism of thought implied in their conflict. The victory of form is no mere technical achievement; it has, as has form in all great art, a spiritual aspect and significance.

It is the development from *Troilus and Cressida* to the latest group of plays that gives to both their profoundest meaning. Our understanding of the latest plays bears strict equivalence with our understanding of this one; only so far as we imagine the abomination of desolation can we imagine beatitude. For the tragedies that follow represent a recovery of the balance between the perception of evil and a positive interpretation of it,[1] whereas in *Troilus and Cressida* the writer looks upon the implacable fact of orderless evil in the mind and in the objective universe alike. In this play the judgement is unshaken, and there is no escape from the torment of the perception of evil, but in the later plays judgement is superseded. The conclusions from all

[1] See Chapter VII below : ' The Equilibrium of Tragedy '.

F

its experiments meet in the tense yet motionless equilibrium
of Troilus's last speech, but the revelations perceived by the
mode of thought that supersedes it flash out in sudden
phrases on the lips of Edgar, Gloucester, and Lear :

> Sit gods upon your thrones, and smile at Troy.
> I say at once, let your brief plagues be mercy,
> And linger not our sure destructions on. . . .
> I do not speak of flight, of fear, of death,
> But dare all imminence that gods and men,
> Address their dangers in. . . . But march away :
> Hector is dead : there is no more to say.

' Let your brief plagues be mercy ' ; Edgar in *Lear* learns at
length that ' the worst is not, So long as we can say this is
the worst ', and his discovery rests upon the knowledge,
carried over from *Troilus and Cressida*, that when we are at
the worst ' there is no more to say'.

In the next phase of this experience, then, there is no
longer this vigilant judgement presiding over implacable
fact, for a break-up has set in and disintegration has over-
powered judgement. In the picture offered by *Timon*, the
play which appears to reveal the next phase in this progression, the universe of thought and imagination is riven
almost beyond recognition and the matter and form of the
play derive from the experience, not of imminent disjunction,
but of chaos itself. This brings its own anæsthesia and,
though the powers of the mind seem to have surrendered to
disintegration, something that was invisible at the stage of
Troilus and Cressida is beginning to appear. The ' strong
base of the world' has indeed now broken up, but through
the rift is revealed, at depths almost below man's vision, a
new base not dreamed of, where the ' perpetual-sober gods '
remain, untouched even by the ' trepidation of the spheres '.
The emergence from destructive to constructive experience
has begun again, though it may be revealed in *Timon* only
in this one phrase. Our experience of each play is, I venture
to think, incomplete without the other.

In *Lear* the indications of this are more frequent and the
conversions that flow in rising and cumulative waves through
the last two acts of the play all set towards a positive, though
undefined, interpretation, resting upon this foundation.

The tragic balance is readjusted. The perception of evil is as full as in the *Oedipus* or the *Oresteia*, but there is an undefined, but no less positive, perception of order emerging again from casualty.

Glouc.   O you mighty Gods !
This world I do renounce, and, in your sights,
Shake patiently my great affliction off;
If I could bear it longer, and not fall
To quarrel with your great opposeless wills,
My snuff and loathed part of nature should
Burn itself out.
.   .   .   .   .   .
You ever gentle Gods, take my breath from me,
Let not my worser spirit tempt me again
To die before you please.
.   .   . What are you ?
Edgar. A most poor man, made tame to fortune's blows
Who, by the art of known and feeling sorrows,
Am pregnant to good pity.

There is, of course, no actual refutation of the conclusions of *Troilus*. The commentary of *Lear* is rather a series of flashes out into a seemingly limitless universe of positive ideas and the later plays extend and stabilize these. But this kind of commentary does, by its very non-logical process, indicate in part how the universe of *Troilus* was superseded. The brief visions of circumambient reality, the ' perpetual-sober Gods ', the ' great opposeless wills ', the ' ever-gentle Gods ', suggest that the imagination may in this way perceive what, in the earlier play, operating in a field of actuality delimited by the judgement, it could not; Edgar could, if he chose, refute Ulysses' argument, that intrinsic value can never become effective because man's judgement is preoccupied with assessed value, by pointing out that it contains an undistributed middle on the grand scale.

Simultaneously there comes into sight that earlier mood again in which,

There's not the smallest orb which thou beholdest
But in his motion like an angel sings,
Still quiring to the young-eyed cherubins;
Such harmony is in immortal souls.

and that, slightly later, in which Pericles, in face of the opening vision of a universe of fundamental order and reconciliation, finds again the image in which Shakespeare has clothed this idea, whether negative or positive, throughout :

Per.   . . . But what music ?
Hel.   My Lord I hear none.
Per.   None ? The music of the spheres.

Already we are in sight of the harmony of the latest plays, and the seeming finality of the vision of *Troilus and Cressida* is seen to be, after all, not an end, but the birth of a new, infinitely extended and positive vision. At the phase at which Lear completes and resolves the experience of Troilus and Cressida, only the anticipation of this is indicated. *Plus ultra.* ' It is enough that there *is* a beyond.'

CHAPTER FIVE

THE FUNCTIONS OF IMAGERY IN DRAMA

THE three plays or groups that we have already considered have shown how seemingly incompatible subject-matter may be shaped into dramatic form, a supreme work of art winning a victory, where least expected, by transcending the normal limitations. But victory of this kind on the grand scale is rare, and there are less remarkable triumphs over limitation which are made possible by skilful and unobtrusive technique. These are almost all matters of detail rather than of basic structure and generally work by extending the scope through suggestion and implication without modifying the presentation of the matter. Imagery and prosody, together with certain bold conventions and even devices of setting, serve in various ways to overcome the disadvantages of that brevity which is essential to the concentration and immediacy of drama. A play in which any or all of these are richly used conveys an impression both of magnitude and of subtlety, while the dramatist who uses fewer of them must (like Ibsen in the social dramas) compensate the resulting austerity by some other means, such as the power and skill of the architecture. It is hardly necessary to point out that the average sound theatre play, whether of the present age or of any other, does neither; its potency is thus commensurate with its necessary dramatic brevity; it may be effective in the theatre, but it will not grow in the mind as will a great imaginative work of art.

Of these ways of deepening the imaginative significance of a play without increasing its length or bulk, imagery is perhaps at once the most simple and the most powerful.[1]

In approaching this question we take almost inevitably as our point of departure the finest poetic drama, such as that of Shakespeare's maturity, in which the imagery seems to be entirely functional. Such imagery, that is to say, is

[1] We should, however, be on our guard against under-estimating the corresponding function of prosody in verse drama.

an integral part of the play, just as is the theme or the structure; it is there, just as they are, because it is essential to the play, because it has a function belonging to nothing else but imagery, because without that imagery the play would be the poorer from whatever aspect we regarded it. At the other extreme from this there are admittedly plays (which perhaps qualify but doubtfully for the title 'poetic') in which such imagery as there is is wholly or partly decorative and not an integral part of the play. There are also many plays, probably the greater number, in which the relation between the whole work of art and the imagery occupies a position intermediate between these two, in which the imagery is at times an aspect of the whole and at other times only incompletely related. But unless we are concerned mainly with the historical side of the subject, with tracing the development of this relation, our interest will almost certainly turn first to those plays in which the functional value of imagery is most fully revealed.

When we speak of imagery in this way we generally find that we are using the term in that stricter and somewhat limited sense which recent writers have tended to adopt when considering Shakespeare,[1] taking it, that is, either as co-extensive with metaphor or at most with the figures closely allied to metaphor. This is, I believe, advisable, even though, in the special case of drama, there are sometimes reasons for extending it to include the frontiers of symbolism, description, or even, it may be, the setting itself, when, as in much modern drama, the playwright relies upon that to express a part of his intention.[2]

Can we, then, within these limits, describe what are or have been some of the functions by which imagery helps drama to overcome the limitations inherent in its brevity?

All imagery that has a functional relation with a play increases dramatic concentration. In common with all genuine metaphorical expression, it reveals a significant and

[1] This, as I interpret them, is the view of H. W. Wells, Middleton Murry, S. J. Brown, Elizabeth Holmes, C. F. E. Spurgeon, G. W. Knight, and Wolfgang Clemen, among others.
[2] A familiar instance is the work of H. Lenormand in the present century.

suddenly perceived relation between an abstract theme and a subject closer to the experience of the senses in such a way as to transfer to the rightly apprehending mind the shock, the stimulus with which the union of these two stirred the mind of the poet himself. Strong emotional experience is stored in the brief space of an image, and its release illuminates powerfully the emotions, the reflections, the inferences which it is the purpose of the passage to evoke. There is thus an artistic economy in imagery hardly to be equalled by that of any other kind of verbal expression, with the possible exception of irony; in each the potency comes from the high charge of implicit thought or feeling. Moreover, dramatic imagery tends to be the most strongly charged of all kinds; the concentration natural to drama impressing itself upon the imagery, just as the imagery in its turn enables the drama to increase its native concentration.[1]

A play which contains little or no imagery is not necessarily shorter than a play which carries a high charge of it. The concentration of imagery in a poetic play operates rather by enabling the play, without overrunning its brief form, to extend its scope and strengthen its texture. Lacking the leisure and the digressive privileges of the narrative and reflective forms, drama is sometimes in danger of poverty of implication or detail. This is true even of the finest type of drama, which maintains severely its proportioning and the magnitude of its theme. Even here, without the support of functional imagery, there is danger of thinness of character, absence of suggestive comment and lack of passionate significance in spite of richness of event. More often than we should readily believe, we find the presence or absence of imagery to be the immediate technical explanation of those differences in content, in fullness and in amplitude in plays otherwise similar in dimension, theme and structure.[2]

[1] Moreover, as Mr. Robert Nichols has recently pointed out to me, a high proportion of the imagery in Shakespeare's plays is dynamic and is distinct in this from the static imagery of the sonnets. Here again is reciprocity : action, which is characteristic of Elizabethan drama, is reflected as movement in the functional imagery of that drama.

[2] An example or two may help to make this clear. Ibsen largely (though by no means entirely) discards imagery (as distinguished from symbolism) in *The Pillars of Society* and the succeeding social plays.

Imagery, as we have said, has certain functions which can compensate drama for the heavy liabilities inherent in its form. Without losing the intensity and compactness which is its virtue, the poetic drama of Aeschylus, of Shakespeare or of one of the modern poetic dramatists, such as Synge, depends largely upon functional imagery for its breadth and scope, for our awareness of a wider setting than that in which the actual events occur. Again, while still preserving its rapidity of pace, drama may, by virtue of the charge carried by its imagery, achieve some of the fullness and elaboration of detail in the revelation of character or of thought which, in narrative or reflective verse and prose, can be revealed at leisure by the descriptive method.

These several functions may be seen at work in the Greek drama as in that of the Elizabethans, at intervals in the drama of the Continent down to the present day and in England again since the revival of the poetic drama in the twentieth century.

Imagery, in such drama, often reveals the presence of a surrounding or accompanying universe of thought or experience which cannot otherwise be included, however essential to its poetic purpose, without forfeiting the rapidity and compression in which the artistic strength of drama chiefly lies. This is often also effected by symbolism, setting or incidental description,[1] but imagery, in the strict sense of

---

But he achieves strength of texture by that close interlocking of event and character that cost him so many revisions. Mr. Eliot, in *The Family Reunion*, to take an opposite case, derives great extension of scope from a specialized use of imagery. Galsworthy's *Strife* appears to separate the two functions, obtaining a certain strength of texture by methods not unlike Ibsen's and a certain enriching of meaning by the images of a few of his characters. But in Shakespeare's work both scope and texture are served by imagery, and the plays would be knit together by it even if the structure were unsure.

[1] We may remind ourselves here of the recurrent symbolism of Ibsen, Strindberg, or Maeterlinck, the fragmentary allegory and personification in the early Elizabethans, and the dreams and visions in the work of some of the Jacobeans (notably of Webster and Tourneur); of the expressionism of Strindberg and the succeeding German school, represented in our own day by Toller and Kaiser; of the setting which itself becomes an image of a mental state in parts of *Macbeth, Lear*, or *Timon*, or in such contemporary plays as Mr. O'Neill's *Emperor Jones*, M. Lenormand's *Simoun, A L'Ombre du Mal* and, somewhat similarly,

metaphorical speech, is a more powerful means; more passionate than symbolism, more flexible than setting, more concentrated than descriptive digression.

This function of imagery may be traced in many of Shakespeare's plays, where the vastness of the issues involved, of which the action that is shown us is but a part, is kept constantly before us by the imagery. As early as *Romeo and Juliet* the vastness of love is illuminated for a moment by an image whose revelation remains with us throughout the sequent action :

> My bounty is as boundless as the sea,
> My love as deep.

Just so, the universal, all-enveloping horror of Macbeth's crime, its unutterable and inescapable consequence, is borne in upon us, not only by the pitiless relation of cause and effect revealed in the action, but by images that light up, by potent analogy, the nature of the deed :

> This my hand will rather
> The multitudinous seas incardine
> Making the green one red.

Macbeth's mind, in which ' function is smothered in surmise ', is a microcosm of the ' state ' whose ordered processes are, by the consequences of his deeds, as surely smothered. He thinks instinctively of ' the seeds of time ' and ' Nature's germens ', thus flashing before us in single images the surrounding universes of time and of causality through which the events move.

In Timon's mind the themes of disease, misgeneration, and robbery image themselves in the elements ; the earth, the sea, and the great processes of nature. We are never long

---

in *Le Temps est un Songe* and *L'Homme et ses Fantômes*. (A detail similarly used to excellent ironic effect in our own realistic drama is the firescreen at the beginning of Galsworthy's *Strife*.) We may finally notice how incidental description plays this part in many of the early Elizabethans, most gracefully perhaps in the work of Peele. All these fulfil the function of extending the experience of the reader beyond the actual events, passions, and thoughts presented in the play to include a wider experience equally necessary to a full understanding of what is contained within the play.

without this reminder of the universal nature of calamity
and evil :

> The sun's a thief and with his great attraction
> Robs the vast sea; the moon's an arrant thing
> And her pale fire she snatches from the sun.

In *Troilus and Cressida* again there is constant reference
out from the affairs of man, in which the action consists, to
the surrounding universe of being to which they transfer
and from which they derive their sickness.   The polity of
man mirrors the order or disorder of the cosmos, and universal
disjunction and disintegration are there imaged with a
rapidity and power that could not be compassed in long
passages of descriptive analysis.   Much of the tempest
imagery in *Lear* has a like function.

In *Antony and Cleopatra* there is brought before us by the
imagery first the world-wide power of Rome and of Antony,
' the triple pillar of the world ', and later the presence of the
infinity of time and space which dwarf that world.   For
Cleopatra there is

> Nothing left remarkable
> Under the visiting moon.

while, in the memory of Antony,

> His voice was propertied
> As all the tuned spheres.

Her longings are ' immortal ', and Charmian has leave to
play till doomsday.[1]

If we look for a modern parallel to these we may find
something similar in Synge's peculiar use of nature imagery,
especially in his later plays, in which it suggests the world
surrounding the action but not directly presented in it.
This is especially noticeable in *The Playboy of the Western
World*, where it reveals the background of the characters
and their actions.   Synge does not attempt, like Aeschylus
and Shakespeare, to reveal a vast, surrounding world of
being.   He contents himself with using it (most precisely) to

[1] These images are not incidental or scattered, as may be suggested
by so brief an indication, but constant and frequent, forming, in all
these plays and in many others, continuous motives or undertones.
(C. F. E. Spurgeon notices, to take a specific case, that in *Antony and
Cleopatra* there are no fewer than forty-two recurrences of the word
' world ' in the imagery.   See *Shakespeare's Imagery*, p. 352.)

reveal an accompanying, but separate part of the experience of his characters.[1] Its presence is an essential part of the natures of the people and of their conduct. That they are, unlike the people in *Riders to the Sea*, unaware of the moulding power of the world outside Flaherty's shebeen, adds subtlety and significance to the functional power with which Synge invests their unconscious references and images. The dialogue is full of brief pictures, either in description or in metaphor, of the empty, isolated, and yet beautiful country-side of Mayo. Inside the bar are the drunken peasant farmers with their dreary lives and their starved but in-flammable imaginations. The desolation of the country has crushed their enterprise, its beauty has kept their imagina-tions living. Out of the conflict comes their aptitude for intoxication, whether by the liquor of Kate Cassidy's wake or by the saga of Christy Mahon's heroic exploit. Synge has presented in the setting of the play the inside of the shebeen, only one of the two worlds they live in. He has thrown upon the imagery and allusions the entire function of revealing a world outside, by which this has been conditioned.

But these are only various forms of one function of imagery, that which reveals the relations between the world of the play and a wider surrounding world or universe. Far more frequent in poetic drama are those functions by which imagery enriches the content and implications that lie within the play itself. And of these perhaps the most frequent is that which reveals or keeps in mind the under-lying mood. This not only knits the play together but emphasizes by iteration—and by iteration whose appeal is always to the emotions—the idea or mood which had guided the poet's choice of theme and shaping of form. It may be urged that this second function of imagery must always be at work in any poetic drama which has become a complete work of art; the main preoccupation of the poet's mind must be revealed in greater or less degree by all the aspects of a play that is the issue of that preoccupation. And it is true that iterative imagery, the peculiar function of which is to keep the dominant mood of the whole before us throughout

[1] See, on Synge's nature imagery and its functions, my *Irish Dramatic Movement*, Chapter VIII.

the succession of parts, may be found, in some degree, in any work in which the poet's expression has issued in full artistic expression. But this, in special cases, becomes so clear as to form a continuous and recognizable undertone throughout the play; the undertone of moonlight and woodland in *A Midsummer Night's Dream*, of light and darkness in *Romeo and Juliet*, of sound and movement in *Much Ado About Nothing*.[1]

The function here is clear. A play is fuller and richer in significance because we are continually in the presence of certain elements in nature, themselves the reflection of the mood in which the play is written. This kind of imagery is distinct from, though it may harmonize with, setting or its Elizabethan equivalent, incidental description. For though the subjects of the images may seem to reproduce the setting, as in *A Midsummer Night's Dream*, much of their potency derives from the fact that they *are* images, called forth not by the immediate need to represent a scene but primarily in response to the poet's perception of a fundamental identity between them and his theme. When Lorenzo exclaims, " How sweet the moonlight sleeps upon this bank ! ' we recognize it as a direction to the Elizabethan audience to imagine the setting that could not be presented; it is perhaps hardly more significant than the finest of modern moonlight effects. But when Othello says,

> It is the very error of the moon.
> She comes more near the earth than she was wont
> And makes men mad,[2]

the passage is suffused with a spellbound bewilderment, half of enchantment, half of nightmare, like that which sometimes

---

[1] This has been revealed by the full and lucid analysis of Professor Caroline Spurgeon, to whom I am indebted for the summaries above. See ' Shakespeare's Iterative Imagery ' (*British Academy Proc.*, 1931) and *Shakespeare's Imagery* (Cambridge, 1935), especially Part II, ' The Function of Imagery as Background and Undertone in Shakespeare's Art '.

[2] It may be questioned whether this is strict imagery. Whether it is or not must depend upon the extent to which we credit Othello with a literal belief in the influences of the heavenly bodies upon human destiny. If we assume in him the qualified belief common to many Elizabethans, the ' influences ' would already have become half allegorical and the words therefore metaphorical. It is so that I take them.

follows the awakening from deep unconsciousness into the
strange radiance of moonlight. Othello's mind is revealed
to us in one brief piece of metaphorical illumination, the moon
linking his vision of oncoming madness with the familiar,
cognate physical experience in which it is imaged. In just
such a way, the iterative imagery of moonlight in *A Midsummer Night's Dream* has, because it *is* imagery, the power
to release associations of far fuller content than could be
achieved by a long expository analysis. The picture of
virginity, ' Chanting faint hymns to the cold, fruitless moon ',
illuminates with its implications and charged associations a
play whose central action is a tangle of cross-purposes and
apparent frustrations in love.

Closely related with this service, that of qualifying and
enriching each part of a play by continually recalling the
mood or preoccupation from which all derive, are certain
functions whereby imagery helps to amplify, to make subtler
and more detailed the nature or relation of events, the bases
of character, the content or processes of thought, which might
else suffer impoverishment from the rapidity and compression
of the dramatic form.

In the opening scenes of a play in which events are to
move swiftly we often find a kind of anticipation, not only
of the mood of the subsequent action, but of the very events
themselves; some hint, in the subject of an image, of the
course of the action, which, though we may not notice it
consciously, sinks into the mind and prepares us to accept
more rapidly some series of events which is to follow.
This is a genuine dramatic function; imagery, that is to
say, which is thus used in drama is functional to a high
degree.

One of the Jacobean poetic dramatists, John Webster,
seems to have developed almost consciously this function of
imagery; we may notice that the action of his plays is of
precisely that copious and rapid kind which most needs such
aids as this if it is to maintain depth and significance. In
the first scene of his *Vittoria Corombona*, where the fate of
Lodovico reveals in miniature the passions and forces at work
on the main action of the play, the speeches are shot with
imagery that is prophetic not only of those passions, but of

the kinds of events which they may (and in fact do) draw
down :

> Fortune's a right whore :
> If she gives ought she gives it in small parcels,
> That she may take away all at one swoop.

This is a not unusual Elizabethan image and it is only one of
many that might have satisfied Lodovico's hatred of fortune,
but it is not insignificant that one of the first words that rings
out distinctly in this scene is ' whore ', which is to be bandied
to and fro around Vittoria through the rest of the play and
sums up one interpretation of the main part of the action.
And the swoop of destruction is the fit image of the sudden
turns of fortune and of the final catastrophe.   Fortune in the
later part of this image has already become in part a bird or
beast of prey.   In the next lines Lodovico's ' great enemies '
become ' your wolf ', the fitting embodiment of the predatory
and ruthless figure of Flamineo, who guides and twists the
action to his ends, only himself to founder in swift-moving
destruction.   ' An idle meteor ', Gasparo calls Lodovico, to
be ' soon lost i' the air ' ; and we have another image of the
later action, in the brilliant and blazing careers of Vittoria,
Brachiano, Flamineo, which vanish into sudden extinction,
' driven I know not whither '.   And the images from knives,
swords, and daggers here, ' I'll make Italian cut-works in their
guts ', ' Great men sell sheep thus to be cut in pieces ', point
on with sinister precision to the details of the final havoc.[1]

Sometimes a still subtler form of this use may be found
in Shakespeare's works.   In the first and third scenes of
Cymbeline there is a series of images connected with or spoken
by Imogen, which unobtrusively conveys her isolation, her
exposure to the pricks of malice and of evil eyes,[2] and does
this more quickly and more fully than would much direct

---

[1] These are only a few of the images that are, I think, charged with
this power of anticipating by pictures or associations the nature of the
events that follow.   The same functional use can be found in the
opening scene of Webster's second play, *The Duchess of Malfi*, in both
of Tourneur's (especially the *Revenger's Tragedy*) and, in an elementary
form, as early as Marston's *Antonio and Mellida*.   It was, I think, well
understood (though not necessarily consciously understood) among
many of the dramatists of the early Jacobean period.

[2] ' Evil-eyed ', ' tickle ', ' wounds ', ' hourly shot of angry eyes ',
' gall ', ' a pinch . . . more sharp ', ' a touch more rare ', ' needle ',
' prick ', ' sharp as any needle ', ' gnat ', etc.

comment from other characters. By helping so to convey
her position, it helps also to convey the balance of the situation, the hostility surrounding her, upon which much of the
subsequent action depends.

Closely akin to this use, though probably more usual and
possibly more powerful, is the aid given by imagery to the
rapid and significant revelation of character. How much
more impressive and vivid are the brief imagistic summaries of
character given at the beginning of *The Duchess of Malfi*
than, for instance, Ben Jonson's lucid and often exquisitely
balanced character analyses in *Cynthia's Revels*. How much
deeper, indeed, than the impression made by these intellectual expositions is that of the imaginative picture of Ben
Jonson's own Volpone?

> A fox
> Stretched on the earth, with fine delusive sleights,
> Mocking a gaping crow.

This, or some part of the picture called up by it, stays in the
memory for the rest of the play and guides us, quicker than
pages of character study, to the right interpreting of Volpone's character in the action which immediately follows.
Just such is the function of the image, in *The Duchess of
Malfi*, which introduces the Cardinal and Ferdinand; they
are ' plum-trees that grow crooked over standing pools;
they are rich and o'er-laden with fruit, but none but crows,
pies, and caterpillars feed on them '.

In all these the function of revealing character has fallen
upon the associations of the subject in which it is imaged.
But there is another and sometimes subtler use of image
which occurs also in a large number of the Jacobean
dramatists. In this the characters reveal themselves by
their instinctive choice of subjects in which to image their
thought and often also by the form of the image, by the
relation, that is, between subject and theme. The work of
Webster, Tourneur, and Shakespeare is full of imagery
which has this profoundly dramatic function.[1] Shakespeare's

---

[1] C. F. E. Spurgeon has made a detailed analysis of the imagery of
Falstaff, showing in what ways and to what extent it reveals his character (*Shakespeare's Imagery* : Appendix VII). It will be seen in this
examination that the character could be reconstructed from the images
alone, with their revelation of the content of the mind.

later characters, and in some degree those of his middle
period, have their individual imagery.   It is related inevitably
to the underlying mood out of which the play is, like the
characters, generated, but is yet subtly distinguished, within
the limits of that character's relation to the whole.   Hamlet,
Claudius, and Gertrude; Macbeth, Lady Macbeth, Macduff,
Ross, and even the murderers have their own trend of
imagery in subject or in form or in both; so again have
Timon, Lear, Edmund, Antony, Cleopatra, Prospero.[1]

The imagery of Claudius and Gertrude furthers, without
our necessarily being aware of the means, our understanding
both of their characters and of their relationship.   Indeed,
certain of the ' problems ' of the play might with advantage
be referred to the findings of a detailed analysis of these two
significant groups.   A brief indication of their function may
perhaps serve here to indicate the value of the direct and
unobtrusive revelation of character which can be made by
imagery.   The imagery of Claudius's public speech differs
from that of his speech in private, though there are some
fundamental resemblances.   On formal occasions it is brief,
superficial, and commonplace, illustrating his statements in
a clear, efficient way that is hardly ever imaginative.   The
subjects of the images are homely, drawn from everyday life,
frequently from warfare or military life, and sometimes from
the operations of justice.   He seldom surprises us by revealing anything beneath this surface, though he can sometimes,
as in endeavouring to conciliate Laertes, become inept.[2]

----

[1] I have instanced here only a few out of many characters.   Upon
some of these, and upon others that I have not cited, see Wolfgang
Clemen : *Shakespeare's Bilder*, especially pp. 149–51, 176–79, 207–11,
222–24.

[2]   The great love the general gender bear him;
          Who, dipping all his faults in their affection,
          Would, like the spring that turneth wood to stone,
          Convert his gyves to graces.   (IV, vii.)

This is the result of an over-anxious effort to persuade and convince.
And Shakespeare had doubtless observed that this effort sometimes
causes even so astute an intelligence as Claudius's to lose itself in words.
Claudius seldom uses extended metaphors, and I know of no other
passage in which he has constructed one whose two sides are not aptly
related.   The changing of wood into stone by a petrifying spring is a
highly unsuitable picture of the transforming of Hamlet's punishment
into additional grace or charm by the affection of the people.   If it

In private life, when he is alone, with Gertrude whom he can deceive easily or with certain courtiers such as Polonius whom he deceives hardly less easily, it is more vigorous and reveals more and more of the obsessions against which he struggles. It is still simple and generally homely, the index of a mind that is astute and practical rather than speculative or imaginative. But it is no longer superficial or per-functory. The disturbance and sickness of his mind be-trays itself in ever-recurring images of pestilence, infection, poison, and disease, especially hidden disease that feeds on the ' pith of life ', to reveal itself suddenly. The habit of concealment and the dread of discovery find their release in images of painting and false colouring like that of the ' harlot's cheek '; sin is ' rank ' and ' smells to heaven '.

In Gertrude's speech there are remarkably few images, and those generally colourless and drawn almost entirely from commonplace themes. They have little vigour and hardly ever call up a vivid picture : the images of a mind that has never received sharp or deep impressions, that is, in fact, incapable of any imaginative effort. Some light is perhaps thrown upon the boundaries of these two natures and of the place at which they meet by even a cursory glance at the mental habits revealed by the images.

Most, as I have suggested, of the characters of Shake-speare's maturity will be found to have in some degree their native imagery. The contrast between that of Macbeth and Lady Macbeth is too clear to justify a brief examination; a full study of each character could, like Miss Spurgeon's picture of Falstaff,[1] be built up from the images alone. Even in subsidiary characters or in those which closely resemble each other, some traces of individual imagery can be found, contributing, whether we recognize it or not, to our

---

says anything, it says the opposite of what Claudius would have it mean—the inflexible stone replacing the live and flexible wood is a process the reverse of that by which the encumbering fetters add to Hamlet's graces.

I have examined this one passage in some detail because, taken in conjunction with the rest of Claudius's imagery in public speech—plain and straightforward as it usually is—this is a delicate indication of the fumbling uncertainty of his mind in this scene.

[1] See above, p. 87.

G

quicker apprehension of their distinctive qualities; in the speech of Regan there is a slight preponderance of images drawn from calculation, wealth contrasted with poverty; in that of Goneril a similar preponderance of images drawn from passion and the uncurbed experience of the senses. In the speech of Edmund, images from disease and maiming conflict (especially at the beginning of the play) and alternate with those drawn from the elemental energies of nature, and both are crossed again by others, from the exercise of skill, of adroit and successful manipulation. With him, as with Claudius, the native strain is stronger in solitude and subdued or disguised in public.

The same poetic revelation of character and mental pre-occupation may be traced in dramatists of far more limited range than Shakespeare, who are also, within their limits, capable of nice distinctions in this field. One of the most consciously precise of his contemporaries is Cyril Tourneur, whose *Atheist's Tragedy* offers a group of characters all differentiated by this means. In spite of Tourneur's con-scious psychological exposition, a great part of our under-standing of the characters is actually due to our largely unconscious assimilation of what is revealed by their images. D'Amville's character, the most potent and virile in the play, is revealed in outline by his actions and his cogent and fiery commentary; but in the last analysis it is mainly to the subjects and the form of his images that we owe an impression of a character in which power of imagination has been deliberately balanced by the playwright against a scientist's approach to and treatment of fact. Brief but highly charged poetic images are followed by the lucid, often sustained illustrative or intellectual imagery in which Tourneur delighted.[1] In marked contrast with D'Amville's is the imagery of Sebastian in the same play; plain, pithy, and with excellent relating of theme to subject, but the imagery of a

[1] Special reference may be made to certain passages : *The Atheist's Tragedy*, II, iv, 104–8, 203–4, IV, iii, 244–58, and V, i, 94–100. For a fuller analysis of Tourneur's imagery in a somewhat different connec-tion, see my article, ' The Imagery of *The Revengers Tragedie* and *The Atheist's Tragedie* ', *The Modern Language Review*, July 1935, and for his use of imagery to reveal character, mood, and temperament see my *Jacobean Drama*, pp. 160–61.

shrewd and energetic practical mind. In marked contrast again is that of Levidulcia, which, in addition to being voluble and commonplace, shows a loose linking of subject and theme, not in a single instance and to indicate a momentary uncertainty, as with Claudius, but so constantly that we realize it as the very habit of her mind. Her conduct throughout the play testifies to a slipshod mental process; the structure of her own images reflects it.[1]

This, which is one of the most important of the dramatic functions of imagery, is frequent in the Elizabethan drama. It can be traced in much other poetic drama, whether in verse or prose, but falls into abeyance, as does all living imagery of whatever function, in prosaic and naturalistic drama. It returns, as do those other kinds, with the revival of poetic drama in our own century, though the absence of live metaphor in the common speech of our time has an inevitable reaction upon the language of our drama and upon the playwright's choice of themes and characters. A conscious and deliberate use of imagery to fulfil this and other cognate functions is to be found in certain kinds of analytical drama, in expressionist drama, especially when this approaches surrealist technique, and in plays of specific psychological theme. But even in these it is less abundant, I think, than in the drama of the great poetic period; Strindberg, Kaiser, and O'Neill (to instance only a few) do not use it so amply as the Elizabethans.

There is yet another function of dramatic imagery which, though less usual than those we have already considered, is still of great service in giving fullness of content despite dramatic compression; that in which imagery does the work of argument or reflection. A discussion or process of deduction may appear full or complete without the tedious and undramatic dilation that we should at once observe if it were in fact complete. In Hamlet's soliloquies imagery, rather than abstract terminology, is generally the medium for the expression of reflection, and when he speaks of ' the native

[1] This culminates and is best illustrated in the soliloquy before her suicide, where the confusion between the various rivers, fountains, and oceans and their relation to the passions and deeds that they are called upon to image defy elucidation. There is, of course, no question but that Tourneur's art here is conscious and deliberate.

hue of resolution ' as ' sicklied o'er with the pale cast of
thought ', we apprehend in two brief lines a condition of mind
which would need many lines or indeed speeches were it to
be expounded. And so, throughout the soliloquy, moods and
states of mind are revealed by single images or groups and
related to each other by the apposition of the images and the
transitions from one to another. The effect of a long psychological diagnosis is thus given in one speech, without diluting
the dramatic concentration.

In certain other passages in Shakespeare's plays [1] the way
in which the images are placed in relation to each other
implies a train of thought linking image with image which is,
upon analysis, found to be itself an argument. The original
train of thought is thus started afresh in the minds of an
audience who can catch the successive implications of the
images, so that at the end of the speech they have experienced
the equivalent of a long argument in the compass of a relatively brief speech, simply by virtue of the power with which
imagery is charged to stimulate and to illuminate the
imagination. Almost the whole of the conversation between
Achilles and Ulysses (*Troilus and Cressida*, III, iii) is of this
kind; imagery is used by both speakers (but chiefly by
Ulysses) not only to express single reflections but also to
imply the relationship between a sequence of reflections.
This is perhaps most clear in Ulysses' central speech (III,
iii, 145–90), where the transition from image to image—from
the oblivion caused by ungrateful Time to perseverance which
' keeps honour bright ', from past virtue, which is ' to hang
Quite out of fashion ' to the fierce competition of the narrow
way of honour—give by the shock of their juxtaposition, the
stimulus which stirs the imagination not only to apprehend
the image but to apply the inferences to which these deliberately contrasted images are designed to lead us. Though
this function appears perhaps most frequently and most

---

[1] Upon a cognate but slightly different use of imagery as a general
medium for reflection in Shakespeare see Wolfgang Clemen : *Shakespeare's Bilder* (Bonn, 1936), Section ii, ' Reflexion in Bildern '. ' Bilder ',
according to Clemen, ' werden mehr und mehr zu einer Hilfe der
Gedanken der Menschen, zu einer bedeutsamen Kristallisation ihres
Nachdenkens ' (p. 105). And see also Section III, especially pp. 131–32,
149–51.

powerfully in *Troilus and Cressida*, that play is by no means alone in this respect. Parts of *Hamlet* and much of *Measure for Measure* on the one hand and of *Timon* on the other depend for their effect upon this function.

In reflective and in religious poetry we often find images used not only (as in Hamlet's speech) to express an idea, but also to reveal spiritual experiences which, it would appear, could not have been expressed (or not by that writer) in the language of abstract statement. When Wordsworth says,

> For I must tread on shadowy ground, must sink
> Deep—and, aloft ascending, breathe in worlds
> To which the heaven of heavens is but a veil,

we are in the presence of imagery of this kind. Sometimes, but not often, drama enters this territory, and when it does we often find that it is to imagery that the poet turns as the quickest and most potent—sometimes, it may be, the sole— means of expressing a thought impossible to convey in disquisition or in action unless these were intolerably and undramatically extended. When Chapman's Byron in the hour of death reflects that he is seated ' betwixt both the heavens ', he takes leave of the world in a series of pictures which attempt to image the approaching disintegration of the mind in death, an experience which neither Chapman nor his hero would have found easy to expound or to analyze in abstract terms :

> Wretched world,
> Consisting most of parts that fly each other,
> A firmness breeding all inconstancy,
> A bond of all disjunction ; like a man
> Long buried, is a man that long hath lived ;
> Touch him, be falls to ashes : for one fault,
> I forfeit all the fashion of a man.
> Why should I keep my soul in this dark light,
> Whose black beams lighted me to lose myself ?

Shakespeare's Troilus, revealing to Ulysses his conception of his state, uses imagery in the same way ; his need is in fact even more imperative than Byron's, for, though our imaginations receive his meaning readily enough through the medium of the image, it is hard to give either a clear account of the subject apart from the theme or a statement in abstract

terms of his precise conception of the relations between the
various aspects :

> Oh madness of discourse,
> That cause sets up with and against itself;
> Bifold authority !   Where reason can revolt
> Without perdition, and loss assume all reason
> Without revolt.

In just such a way as this Mr. T. S. Eliot, in *The Family
Reunion*, leaves to imagery the function of revealing much of
the thought or of the spiritual experience which would else
prove well-nigh inexpressible within the limits of dramatic
form.   But the function of the imagery here is even more
vital than in either of the two other cases, for these thoughts
and these experiences are the main stuff of the play,
sometimes its sole action.   Here, then, is a play in which
this peculiar function of imagery is exercised so fully that it
would be hard to find a parallel outside the narrative or
reflective poetry of mystical experience ; yet it is an integral
part of the action and thus essentially dramatic in function :

> There are hours when there seems to be no past or future,
> Only a present moment of pointed light
> When you want to burn.   When you stretch out your hand
> To the flames.   They only come once,
> Thank God, that kind.   Perhaps there is another kind,
> I believe, across a whole Thibet of broken stones
> That lie, fangs up, a lifetime's march.   I have believed this.

This is not incidental description or commentary; it is the
centre of the action because it is the central experience of
the chief characters; it is the subject of the play.

The functions of imagery which we have here considered [1]
are among the most rapid and potent means of deepening
the imaginative significance of a play and thereby helping
to transcend the natural limitations of the form.   Metaphor,

---

[1] Like all students of this subject, I have a considerable debt to the
clear thought and the imaginative analyses of Dr. Clemen's study of
Shakespeare's imagery.   The functions I have considered are not always
those to which he attaches most importance and my categories differ
somewhat from his, while sometimes overlapping.   For his interesting
and exhaustive examination of Shakespeare's early imagery, the reader
is referred to the first part of his book (*Shakespeare's Bilder*), especially
to pp. 30–1, 46, 50, 52, 57, 62, 71, 73, 82, 85–6, 105; for the analysis of
the imagery of the great tragedies, to the later parts, especially sections
III and IV.

being almost inseparable from poetic expression, must find some place in poetic drama and thus, as the art matures, be drawn into closer and closer functional relation. The functions I have tried to indicate here will, I believe, be found to exist whenever poetic drama rises to a height in any way comparable with that of the Greek and of the Elizabethan. (Nor do I doubt that there are other functions that I have not yet discerned in the drama that I have studied and have been unable to experience in that which I have not.) Many, as I have suggested, are already reappearing to-day in the poetic drama of Europe and America, and their presence there appears to indicate the operation of a fundamental law of dramatic aesthetics.

Indeed, that this should be so is not improbable, since the history of dramatic form is in one sense a history of its conflict with its own inherent limitations. That imagery should be one means of circumventing these is, it would appear, as inevitable as that certain technical devices, to be examined in detail in the following chapter, should be evolved for a similar purpose. The conflict of dramatic form with its potential content calls into being the peculiar functions of imagery that have been indicated here. The conflict between content and medium leads to the various devices which must now be considered.

CHAPTER SIX

A TECHNICAL PROBLEM: THE REVELATION OF UNSPOKEN THOUGHT IN DRAMA

ONE of the primary technical characteristics of the dramatic form is the presentation of fact and event through the medium of words spoken by the agents themselves. Except for a few movements deeds, thoughts, and emotions are all communicated to the audience by means of the characters' own statements. And our final impression, after reading a good play, is of statements we willingly believe that people in these circumstances would make; good drama leaves us with a conviction of its essential veracity, whether or not it attempts verisimilitude. It satisfies our sense of what is probable on the emotional level of that particular play.[1]

But this instrument of direct speech, cogent and powerful as it can be, imposes no less surely its own limitations on the content. These limitations each great age of drama tries in its own way to circumvent, break down, or transcend, attempting a resolution of this particular conflict between medium and content. Some of the problems that give rise to this attempt and, more still, some of the ways in which they have been met, throw light on the nature of drama, as well as on the history of this aspect of the general conflict. Familiar to all readers of plays are the problems of exposition (of introducing the audience, that is, to the circumstances of the play); the cognate problems set up by the conflict, throughout the action, of credibility and convention; and the problem of conveying to the audience thought which cannot naturally form part of the dialogue. It is the last

[1] How readily do we detect (to take the simplest instance) a playwright's clumsiness in conveying to us necessary information, no matter how plausibly he manœuvres it into the plot. How often do we find ourselves echoing Sheridan's succinct comment, 'Mr. Puff, as he knows all this, why does Sir Walter go on telling him?' Unnatural dialogue destroys our confidence in the playwright's æsthetic sincerity, no matter what necessity drives him to it; we feel, like Mr. Dangle, that their speech does not spring directly enough from their emotions and circumstances.

of these which has provided perhaps the most interesting succession of solutions.

The medium of direct speech gives to drama a great part of its cogency and power. But a play which communicates to the audience only those passions or thoughts which the characters can communicate naturally to each other is in danger of becoming either superficial or colourless. If the action is at all vigorous, the characters may lack depth or definition; and if, instead, they reveal themselves fully by slow and indirect processes like those of ordinary life, the play may be attenuated into a series of conversation pieces, intellectually subtle, perhaps, but dramatically languid. The dramatist whose interpretation is complex or profound is faced, then, with what seems an insuperable problem. To convey to his audience any considerable part of his own understanding of his character's experience, he must find some further means of communicating with that audience, more rapid and direct than the medium of strict dramatic dialogue. Yet the very nature of his form seems to forbid it. That is why the history of this aspect of dramatic technique reveals a succession of attempts to circumvent this condition or to break through it,[1] to combine fullness or revelation with probability and with concentration.

But the attempt is itself dangerous. In the hands of lesser dramatists circumvention is liable to give way to acquiescence, tolerable in comedy but deadening to tragedy, while the attempts to break through are often destructive of character and probability and so of the very foundations of drama.[2] In the hands of the virtuoso, circumvention, though

---

[1] Only a few highly specialized types of drama, such as the English Restoration Comedy, have been able to achieve high excellence as works of art without attempting to include at least some material naturally intractable to the form.

[2] Comedy that acquiesces in these limitations instead of circumventing them suffers less than tragedy because the very nature of its material allows it to indicate, if it wish, only that part of its character's experience which is immediately concerned with the plot. At its extreme this results in farce, but the comedies of Henry Arthur Jones offer good instances of its normal use. But when tragedy or serious drama thins down the thought and passion to what can be communicated thus, its potency may be lowered, even in a skilfully arranged play (such as Elizabeth Baker's *Chains*). The effects of heedless defiance of the natural limitations of drama, on the other hand, are familiar to

brilliant and subtle, may become an end in itself and trammel
the action of the play,[1] while the process of breaking through
is often more superficially than profoundly original. In the
hands of the great poetic dramatists alone is this inner knowledge of the thoughts of the characters revealed without
sacrificing the ultimate impression of dramatic directness;
fullness of experience is there communicated without loss of
cogency or of truth. In their hands only has another kind
of extension, this time within the framework of the drama,
triumphed over the limitations that the form or the medium
tends to impose on the content.

When we consider the ways in which this problem has been
solved or attacked, we find three or four that are of some
interest : the Greek chorus and later attempts to revive it,
of which Hardy's *The Dynasts* is one of the most notable; the
soliloquy, which is at its height in the English Elizabethan
drama, with a few antecedents in the Greek and in the
medieval European drama and with successors in that of the
seventeenth century in France and in the eighteenth and
nineteenth centuries in Germany; the attempt, for which
Ibsen is mainly responsible in the first instance, to communicate everything by implication and juxtaposition, without breaking through the dramatic form; and a restless
succession of experiments in our own day which can with
difficulty be classified, except in so far as they are all conscious attacks upon this particular limitation and often defeat
themselves by taking undue liberties with form. All except
the third of these kinds have one thing in common; something which in actual life would pass through the mind without being uttered, or even, it may be, formulated, is spoken
aloud by one of the actors. In most great drama it will be
found that audience and playwright collaborate, it may be
unconsciously, in a willing suspension of strict dramatic
effect for the moment in order that the fundamental processes of drama may be the more fully served.

In great poetic drama any such suspension can go to considerable length without disturbing our conviction; the

modern readers, for they are characteristic of much contemporary
writing. (See also below, pp. 120 ff.)
[1] See below, pp. 116 ff.

emotional level is raised and the field of consciousness extended, so that, though we do not mistake a given speech for the words that would be uttered in the actual life we know, we are so deeply engaged by the significant reality that our sense of relative value prevails and we accept without cavil (often without consciousness) some convention such as chorus or soliloquy which, by sacrificing verisimilitude, immeasurably enriches our experience of reality. We often understand better the factors which govern this phenomenon when we come upon a passage in a poor play, generally a melodrama,[1] in which the sacrifice of actuality is made not in the service of greater reality but simply for the convenience of the theatre. Here, defect of imagination or of skill, laziness, or indifference may produce soliloquy, aside, and even dialogue which is neither a record of probable every-day speech nor a significant selection from the thoughts which pass through the mind or move beneath its surface.[2]

We can examine the process itself a little more closely if, taking each of our four kinds[3] in turn, we consider our own response to the technique of various plays.[4]

What happens when we watch (or read as though we were watching it in the theatre) a play of Aeschylus, Sophocles, or Euripides? Do we not distinguish, among the various functions of the chorus when not itself an actor, that of conveying to us an important part of our impression of the significance of the events and of the experiences of the people who themselves create the action? This varies with the varying types of tragedy, distinguishing, as do certain other

---

[1] We sometimes find this more tolerable in farce, where it also occurs (and for the same reason), because we are inclined to accept the amusement derived from the plot as a valid exchange.

[2] Such passages merely invent a formula for telling us quickly what are the main preoccupations and reactions of the characters, so that we may know just enough of the psychological pre-requisites to follow the action. This is the opposite of the procedure of great poetic drama, whether in prose or verse.

[3] See above, p. 98.

[4] I propose to set aside for the moment the question whether the various audiences for whom these plays were intended were at different levels of artistic consciousness and so liable to make different interpretations of dramatic convention. That this was so is, I think, very probable, but it is easy to exaggerate the extent to which it might control or influence the technique of drama.

functions of the chorus, the Old Tragedy from the Middle and the Middle from the New, and one play from another within those groups, especially with Aeschylus and with Euripides; but a re-reading of a few representative plays will reveal this process in some of its manifestations.[1]

The characters in the *Agamemnon*, to take a single instance from the later work of Aeschylus, state what they feel or think (or what they wish their dramatic audience to think they feel or think) in such speech as men and women might use in a state of heightened being; it does not disturb our sense of aesthetic probability. Yet we bring to our apprehension of their tragedy far more awareness of their underlying thought and emotion, a far closer understanding of the significance of their crimes and sufferings than they have themselves conveyed to us. We bring to it something of what is in their subconscious minds, some perception, which we feel has entered their spirits also, of the vast implications of these passions, these memories, these purposes. This enriching of the implications of the words in each speech has not come merely from the relation of those speeches to each other within the framework of the action, important though this factor is. It has come also from something quite apart from this, from certain speeches of the chorus (such as the first choral hymn)[2] where the lyrics become not a direct commentary on or an immediate response to the events or to the declarations of the characters, but an undertone that repeats their theme independently, and, in so doing, draws into significant relation both the outward action of the play and the surrounding universe of moral and spiritual law. If we were to read or produce this play including only those parts in which the actors (or the chorus as actors) take part, we might carry away an impression of hard, sinister, implac-

[1] A complete analysis of this question in relation to the thirty-odd plays and fragments of Greek Tragedy that have survived would need a volume to itself. I am here concerned to indicate only what I believe to have been characteristic of the Greek dramatists' solutions of the problem of expressing the inner experience of their characters. The problem admits of—and demands—a far fuller investigation than I am qualified to make. For much interesting suggestion and criticism that illuminates this topic, I would again refer my readers to H. D. F. Kitto's penetrating study : *Greek Tragedy* (Methuen, 1939).

[2] 160–83.

able event and passion, but not, I think, of those events and these passions made significant by the immensity or the complexity of their relation with another universe of being ; [1] not, in fact, of that on which the ultimate poetic significance of the play depends.

> Zeus, whoever He is, if this
> Be a name acceptable,
> By this name I will call on him.
> There is no one comparable
> When I reckon all of the case
> Excepting Zeus, if ever I am to jettison
> The barren care which clogs my heart.
>
> Not He who formerly was great
> With brawling pride and mad for broils
> Will even be said to have been.
> And He who was next has met
> His match and is seen no more,
> But Zeus is the name to cry in your triumph-song
> And win the prize for wisdom.
>
> Who setting us on the road
> Made this a valid law——
>   ' That men must learn by suffering ',
> Drop by drop in sleep upon the heart
> Falls the laborious memory of pain,
> Against one's will comes wisdom ;
> The grace of the gods is forced on us
>   Throned inviolably.[2]

This is not the sentiment of any of the characters, but neither is it a detached exclamation of the author's. It is the expression of a mood, at once a climate of the mind which envelops the chorus and the atmosphere breathed by the agents themselves. This spiritual awareness is in them all, clearly or dimly, stirring misgiving or aspiration, just as the intellectual awareness described in the later part of the hymn,[3] is present in their memories. It is in this way an intimation of the mingled thought and emotion which forms part of their experience, conscious or half-conscious, acknowledged or denied.

[1] This function of the chorus is closely akin to the similar function of imagery noticed on pp. 80–83 above.

[2] *The Agamemnon of Aeschylus*, translated by Louis MacNeice. Faber and Faber, 1936.

[3] Agamemnon's sacrifice of Iphigeneia at the beginning of war with Troy (184–247).

If we compare a recent trilogy, Mr. Eugene O'Neill's *Mourning Becomes Electra*, with its great prototype, the *Oresteia*, we notice almost at once a certain barrenness, a shrinking of significance in the later play, which may be attributed rather to changes in this function of the chorus than to any other single factor. Mr. O'Neill has taken for his chorus a group of small-town gossips and babblers, admirably realistic, individually distinct, and yet closely enough linked with plot and circumstance to make plausible their continual spying and vigilance. In characteristics and function they are thus utterly unlike the Greek choruses, even of Euripides' tragi-comedies, though one might imagine their equivalents in the Old Comedy. They serve to supply gaps in our information and throw sharp sidelights on the conduct and relations of the characters, but they have laid aside the poetic functions of the corresponding chorus of the *Oresteia*. To turn back from them to the original play is to realize afresh and more profoundly that one of the gravest responsibilities laid upon the earlier chorus was that of communicating to us a body of common thought and feeling without which the dialogue would be bleak and limited, yet which the main actors in those circumstances could never utter themselves. Here, at the outset of dramatic history, is a bold and original solution of one of the fundamental problems inherent in the art that Aeschylus had himself done much to shape; it is, moreover, a solution in terms of the technique that he had himself inherited, though this in no way implies that the solution was inherent in the technique.[1] In so far as the speeches of the chorus are outside the action of the play, in just so far is there an incursion of the non-dramatic, breaking in upon relative actualism that was already growing in his hands. Thought that, though unspoken, is present in the minds of the characters, has been communicated directly from author to audience, not only without undue sacrifice of dramatic

---

[1] The dominant chorus, the single actor and the audience trained in Lyric drama (all parts of his inheritance), presumably left Aeschylus less bound by the demands of realism than most subsequent European dramatists. But this did not necessarily indicate that he should draw from these impediments to the growth of realism in drama the very means by which he deepened and extended its reality.

continuity, but, as we have seen, with immense increase of the potency and scope of the dramatic poetry.

A more precise, though not more potent function is exercised occasionally by other choruses. In the *Oedipus Coloneus* the words spoken during the approach of Polyneices[1] seem not only to express sympathy with Oedipus but to reveal also a part of his thought that he himself has not expressed. The reflections seem to spring from a profound experience of pain that can hardly be assumed to be that of the whole chorus and only by a strange coincidence that of the leader; despite the ' οὐκ ἐγὼ μόνος ', of line 1239, we feel that we have here an imaginative reading by the chorus of the mind of Oedipus, an expression of something in the depth of that mind that he himself must necessarily leave unexpressed. A similar use of the chorus may be traced more frequently in Euripides. In *Medea, Ion, Hippolytus*, and *Bacchae*, to instance a few only, we meet choric speeches which, though they might be interpreted as commentary, deduction or reflection arising from the passions or events, seem rather an amplification or extension of the thought of the main agents and to belong more properly to them than to the speakers. After Medea has resolved upon the death of Jason and his bride (ll. 365–408), there is a sudden leap of thought in the ode that follows, a passionate exultation in the dominant force of woman's spirit. This quality has not so far distinguished the Corinthian ladies who make up the chorus, but it certainly has, throughout, characterized Medea, in whose sub-conscious mind it might well be a half-hidden spring.[2]

Outside the Greek drama, there are surprisingly few plays, except avowed imitations, which use precisely this method of revealing the areas of thought most nearly intractable to dramatic form. There is a clear distinction to be drawn between the Greek use of the chorus, a special figure or group speaking in an agreed, extra-dramatic mode, and various

---

[1] 1211–48, 1556–78.

[2] With this we may compare *Bacchae* (882–97, 994–1010), where the chorus has a similar function but with much clearer definition, since it stands as representative of the spiritual force which is the underlying theme of the play; cf. *Hippolytus* (525–63 and 732–63), *Ion* (452–509).

modern devices which use any character that is at hand to
express thought that is either partly or wholly unconscious
or in some way inhibited. It is characteristic of the pure
chorus that it frankly breaks through the dramatic medium
and, among its many other functions, amplifies our understanding of the characters' thought and emotions, thus
widening and deepening the implications of the drama without noticeably extending its length or sacrificing the immediacy of the parts that are conducted in dialogue. One of the
few modern plays which uses, among others, this method of
combatting the limitations of dialogue is Thomas Hardy's
The Dynasts. The Chorus of the Pities, the commentator
on the action and on the circumnabient universe, plays, as the
author points out in the Preface, a part akin to that of a
Greek chorus.[1] Among its other functions may be found
that of sympathetic revelation or amplification of underlying
thought.

It is a different kind of drama that finds the solution of
unspoken thought primarily in the soliloquy, a drama, preoccupied with individuals, which deepens and extends our
knowledge of the characters' inner experience not so much
by indicating their affinities with a common background of
thought and knowledge or with a surrounding universe,[2] as
by revealing more fully the essence of their individual
thought and emotion. Such soliloquy is rare in Greek
drama[3] and does not reach full development as an instru-

[1] The Chorus of the Pities is wholly conscious of its function as commentator, even to the point of discussing it with the other spirit choruses,
and this distinguishes it from any one group of Thebans, Trojan Women
or Corinthians.

[2] A task which may, as has been suggested (see Chapter V above),
be shared by the imagery.

[3] It is perhaps most common in Euripides. Iphigeneia's monologue
(*Iphigeneia in Tauris*, 344–91) is a virtual soliloquy in which she works
out her thought as she speaks, exploring and discovering what is in her
mind : but even monologues such as this are not frequent. The long
opening speeches of certain plays as a rule do the work of prologues also,
so that our main interest there is not in the personality of the speaker
but in the information conveyed. (This is, I think, the response of the
average reader to the speeches of the Watchman in *Agamemnon*, of the
Pythoness in *Eumenides*, of the peasant in *Electra*, of Electra in *Orestes*, of
Iphigeneia in *Iphigeneia in Tauris*, and of Andromache in *Andromache*.
Strict soliloquy, of course, can occur in a Greek play only before the
chorus has entered or after it has withdrawn.)

ment of the dramatic art until the Elizabethan age in England. And even in the early Elizabethan drama it is still primitive and shows that one-half of its parentage is the explanatory interpolation by means of which unskilled Tudor playwrights had broken through the entanglements of their plots. Much early Elizabethan soliloquy is still used to convey knowledge not only of the inner workings of the mind, but also of other necessary matter, the introduction of which makes the speech still more improbable. But even in the earlier period, a dramatist who uses it in this way will often show, in another part of his play, that he has understood also the subtler and more strictly dramatic function.[1]

But at its finest, as at the height of the Elizabethan period, the soliloquy, by its rapid and profound revelation of thought and passion, serves the very ends of drama. It reveals what we could not otherwise divine of the depths of the speaker's mind, compressing into some twenty lines of vivid illumination what might else have taken the better part of an act to convey. And this is done without a long enough interruption of the dialogue to weaken the general effect of probability. Webster's Cardinal in those two brief intervals when he is alone,[2] speaks words which not only reveal the substance of his preoccupation, but, in their brevity, reticence, and dignity, indicate the very process of his mind. ' How tedious is a guilty conscience ! ' What potency there is, not only

[1] We may compare, in Kyd's *Spanish Tragedy*, Lorenzo's succinct and helpful outline of his intentions and schemes (III, iii, 100–19) with Hieronimo's far more dramatic revelation of the tumult of his mind (III, xii, 1–24). Some twenty years later, Tourneur, who shows acute perception of psychological processes in many of his soliloquies, reverts boldly, but with great effectiveness upon occasion, to the informative prologue-soliloquy (see Vindice's speech, *Revenger's Tragedy*, I, i, 1–53). There is an interesting indication that both audience and dramatist regarded soliloquy as a revelation of unspoken thought in Seneca's time in the beginning of Act II of his *Agamemnon*. It is clear that the sixteen lines spoken by Clytemnestra when the scene opens are not supposed to have been heard by the Nutrix, who enquires ' Quid tacita versas ? ' This would be even more difficult to indicate in a recitation than in a normal dramatic presentation, so that we may perhaps judge the convention to have been generally accepted. (My attention was drawn to this passage by a reference, in another connection, in Clarence W. Mendell, *Our Seneca*, p. 90.)

[2] *Duchess of Malfi* : V, iv, 30–2 and V, v, 1–7.

H

in the understatement of that epithet but in the subdued
form in which his thoughts well up for a moment through
their rigid imprisonment, in those two brief speeches !
Hamlet's soliloquies, again, deepen our understanding not
merely by telling us what is at work in his mind, but by
revealing, in the very sequences and form of the speech, the
processes and demeanour of that mind itself. Some such
double process as this is at work in all the soliloquies of
Shakespeare's mature period, in the best of all his contemporaries, and even, in modified form, in later writers such
as Middleton and Ford.[1]

In all these cases the limitation has been mastered without
checking the dramatic movement. Hamlet, the Cardinal,
Beatrice appear to talk as if they were thinking aloud and we
seem to receive the revelation in a completely natural form.
But it is not naturalistic. Their words are not on the same
plane of communication as those of the dialogue, though we
willingly assume that they are. The law of direct presentation (in terms, that is, of speech natural to those characters
in the given circumstances) has been broken by the very fact
that they speak. No man when alone (not even, I think,
an Elizabethan) would actually utter in words the thoughts
that pass through the minds of these and of many other
characters. Men do not as a rule use speech as a means of
disentangling their thoughts and feelings in private; if
they do so it is generally only for fragmentary sounds partly
below the level of articulate speech. In listening to soliloquies our imaginations accept a kind of communication
differing from that of strict drama and more nearly akin
to that of narrative or lyric. We are listening, not to the
most direct presentation that art can make, but to something
at one remove from this. We make the adjustment without
dispute and are generally unaware of what we are doing,
even after fifty years' training in naturalistic drama. Only

[1] See, for cases of special interest here, Ford : *'Tis Pity*, Giovanni's
soliloquy in I, iii, 1 ff. and Annabella's in V, i, 1 ff., and Middleton :
The Changeling, de Flores soliloquy in II, i, 26–51, Beatrice's in IV, i,
1–17 and V, 1–11, and *Women Beware Women*, Leantio's soliloquy
in I, iii, 1–35. It is perhaps worth noticing that in *The Broken Heart*,
which deliberately studies various kinds of reticence, there is hardly any
soliloquy.

if the dramatist presses his demand too far are we conscious of any disturbance of the form.[1] We may go further and say that the very passage which appears to us a reflection of the character's hidden mental processes is deceptive. For few men, thus disentangling thought and feeling, actually use in their minds the full complement of words or sentences that they would use if they were to speak aloud. Syntax and vocabulary themselves break down in the recesses of the mind, for they are connected with the process of communication and come into action only when communication is part of our intention. Hamlet works out the problem of suicide more formally than many a logician might the early phases of an abstract idea. But we do not notice this when we hear or read, and the limitation is thus transcended without loss of dramatic effect.

In every major dramatist's use of soliloquy for this end we find his own distinctive modification of these interacting factors; rationalization of content varies, and with it the extent to which he trespasses upon our credence or convinces us that we are indeed overhearing a man's actual conversation with himself. In the lesser dramatists, whether of the Elizabethan period or later, the device, even while still serving mainly the purpose of self-revelation, may glide into asides and monologues which approach in tragedy to the

[1] An Elizabethan (even a Jacobean) audience may have been more tolerant than we of an obvious mixture of modes, such as we find in less skilful dramatists; for this would follow naturally for them from the admixture of narrative presentation which was common in medieval drama and in the cruder forms of the late sixteenth century. But as soon as dramatist, or audience, becomes self-conscious or uncertain of his technique, as do some of the nineteenth-century imitators of the Elizabethan drama, the dangers of this bold superseding of dramatic form become clear and we find the dramatist attempting to explain them away to the audience. At one point in the *Cenci*, the Count breaks off his soliloquy to say, ' And yet I need not speak, Though the heart triumphs with itself in words ' (I, i, 138–39). Shelley has realized the improbability of Cenci's soliloquy as literal speech. He is too far from the Elizabethan convention to accept it as a frank breaking of verisimilitude, and perhaps afraid of contamination by contemporary melodrama convention. He attempts, therefore, to render the passage natural and to pretend that Count Cenci is actually speaking aloud, by giving psychological justification for what had never, in its origin, been naturalistic. It is clear that for him the soliloquy has ceased to be an interpolation revealing what would not otherwise be conveyed.

usage of melodrama [1] and in comedy to that of farce.   But
in the major dramatists themselves there is still room for
difference.   In the French drama of the seventeenth century,
represented by Corneille and Racine, the soliloquy is so firmly
established as a convention for revealing rapidly the progress of the characters' thoughts and passions that the
pretence of naturalness is largely discarded.   No one sup-
poses that a character could, at the moment of discovering
it, analyze so coherently and lucidly the elements of his
thought and passion and draw from them, in the brief space
of one speech, the firm and assured conclusion from which
his actions are to spring in the next phase of the play.[2]
Such a use of soliloquy discards dramatic illusion, not merely
in the matter of speaking aloud what would mainly be perceived in silence, but, more profoundly, by substituting a
well-wrought, clearly articulated statement, a summary of
the main factors and relations such as might be presented
in a court of law, for the mixture of confusion, misappre-
hension, and sharp illumination which characterizes self-
discovery,   It serves admirably the purpose of acquainting
us rapidly with the motives and springs of the action, but,
though its logical and rhetorical effectiveness is supreme, its
psychological probability is hardly greater than that of the
otherwise far inferior soliloquy of melodrama.   It has
broken through the limitation imposed by the form, but only
at the cost of losing the greatest virtue imposed by that
limitation, the impression of immediacy that derives from
direct speech.   It has solved the most obvious of the technical
difficulties of dramatic writing by temporarily ceasing to be
drama.

Speaking broadly, it may be said that, in the eighteenth

[1] The use of soliloquy and aside in a good melodrama is well worth
examining in this connection.   Henry Arthur Jones' use of it in *The
Silver King*, for example, varies, from the crude device common in
contemporary melodrama to a comparatively subtle revelation of
unspoken thought.

[2] It is well to bear in mind that certain mental habits (lucidity of
thought and fondness for logical procedure) prevail more strongly in
some nations than in others.   Nevertheless, all due allowance being
made for this fact, the processes of Racine's soliloquies still seem in-
humanly coherent and are in contrast to those of Lenormand, J.-J.
Bernard and of other French dramatists at the present day.

and nineteenth centuries, German drama in general treats this function of soliloquy in a way that is closer to the Elizabethans; Lessing, Schiller, and Hebbel, individually distinct as they are, share this affinity. Lessing's people sometimes speak at so high a level of consciousness that they seem to discuss with themselves their own states of mind; only the fact of audible speech, the coherence and the syntactical form of the sentences, remind us that we are not actually sharing a mental debate in which the character disentangles his own reactions to a newly discovered fact or situation.[1] Schiller's characters, again, think aloud, clearing up their reactions, unravelling a situation, reaching a solution and proceeding from that to a resolution, in soliloquies that again are too shapely in emotion and too logical in thought to deceive us once we are familiar with them, though at a first reading Schiller's brilliant theatre technique gives him plausibility precisely where Racine lacked it.[2] Even the soliloquy of Leicester in the fifth act of *Maria Stuart*, which, by an exquisite theatrical device, describes Mary's death, as his imagination pictures it, at the very moment when it is taking place just out of his sight, is psychologically plausible. We accept, without realizing what we are doing, a soliloquy which is at once a revelation of unspoken thought and a ' messenger ' speech; these two functions operate simultaneously without disturbing the effect of dramatic immediacy. In the drama of Hebbel, to take a later writer, the soliloquy (in this function) is still remarkably akin to the Elizabethan use. It reveals the workings of the mind in conflict and self-analysis, and though there is some modification of length or frequency in the later work, there is apparently no vital change in kind.[3]

In Schiller's hands, as in those of the Elizabethans, we suspend disbelief; not, as with Racine, because we accept

[1] This kind of soliloquy is especially frequent in *Miss Sarah Sampson* (III, iv; IV, ii; IV, v), but it can be found also in *Emilia Galotti*.

[2] As, for example, in *Don Carlos* (II, ix; III, v, ix; IV, vi) and *Maria Stuart* (II, vi; IV, iv, x; V, x).

[3] For a careful analysis of Hebbel's treatment of the soliloquy and for the evidence on his own view of it offered by the *Tagebücher*, see Edna Purdie : *Friedrich Hebbel*, pp. 246–48.

some other aesthetic experience in place of that peculiar to
drama, but because he blinds us to the non-dramatic element
in his interpolation.   But when we reach Ibsen we find something akin rather to Shakespeare's own method than to those
even of his contemporaries.   In Ibsen's great soliloquies
convention is, again, but superficial; all beneath is genuine
probability.   Brand, for instance, is a preacher, and the life-
long habit of pulpit argument throbs behind his speech.   He
hammers out his thought into a logical sequence, but we may
remind ourselves that we are watching the self-examination
of a man so trained in that art as to make ordered emotion
and the steady guidance of thought to its conclusion his
second nature.   What we see is not the exaggerated process
of the conventional soliloquy; it is the rooted habit of a
man's mind.   Part prayer, part meditation, part debate, the
soliloquies of Brand are natural (save for the fact that they
are audible) because it is his nature to explore his mind in
ordered, disciplined sequence.   A precisely opposite habit
makes the speech of Peer Gynt equally faithful to his nature.
Brave, fantastic, and boastful speaking is his nature and his
profession; his is the rich and ready imagery of bard and
minstrel.   Words are his instrument, and his delight in his
virtuosity persists when he is alone.   He never plumbs the
recesses of his mind—which is itself a great part of his tragedy.
But his fertile fabrication of dreams is a dominant motive
behind his action, and his soliloquies again have both a
surface of verisimilitude and a core of dramatic truth.   So
hard is it, in fact, to tell when Peer's soliloquies represent
actual speech and when the revelation of unspoken thought,
that there is a wide difference of opinion among Ibsen's
interpreters as to whether he is alive or dead in the fifth act;
whether, that is, the magnificent soliloquies of that act are
the utterances of a half-crazed man stumbling across the fells
or whether they are an extreme use of the convention to
present an image of the experience of the soul after death.[1]

[1] Similar, though not so extreme, instances of the difficulty of
deciding upon the level of consciousness revealed in soliloquy may be
found in many later plays.   We may instance the soliloquy, rendered
as Scene III in Ashley Dukes' translation, in G. Kaiser's *From Morn to
Midnight*.   (The decision is not in either case essential to our apprecia-
tion of the significance of the scene.)

This is in harmony with Ibsen's tendency, in the social dramas, to dispense as far as possible with all conventions.

I have so far omitted all reference to this function in comic soliloquy, because I think it is very rarely exercised except in those cases where comedy itself borders on tragedy and ceases, in fact, to be comedy in anything but name; certain soliloquies are virtually tragic or serious self-revelation like those we have already considered.[1] In passages of genuine comedy, of no matter what age, the people of the drama have a different relation with the audience. In Elizabethan comedy, and to a lesser degree in later forms, it is more natural for the audience to be regarded as a part of the action and so to be taken into the confidence of one or more of the characters without loss of dramatic illusion. When Lancelot Gobbo makes his famous speech [2] directly into the faces of the audience at the foot of the platform, there was, I believe, no risk of his seeming to suspend the action of the play and so of lessening the illusion of the scenes that followed. In a comedy the audience can be treated as bystanders to whom one of the participants appeals for justification, sympathy or support as he might to a crowd in a street. The matter of such comedy is such as might occur in public in everyday life, and the occasional treating of the audience as a crowd who happens to be present increases rather than endangers the impression of immediacy and actuality. Therefore the soliloquy of a comedy can afford to be directed frankly to the audience; it merely implies that one of the interested parties in the events just witnessed has remained behind in the street to express his opinion, his bewilderment, his annoyance or any other state of mind that can readily be shared with the public. Those inchoate passions and explorations of mind which, disguised in one way or another, are the matter of soliloquy in great tragedy are not to be shared with any chance group of bystanders; therefore a convention is used, a break with strict dramatic probability is involved every time they are

[1] Such for example occur in Molière's *L'Avare* (IV, vii) or Middleton's *Chaste Maid in Cheapside* (II, ii, 11–55, and V, i, 67–82).

[2] *Merchant of Venice* (II, ii, 1–34); for an earlier case we may compare Diccon's soliloquy in *Gammer Gurton's Needle* (I, i) and for Molière's own use of this kind of soliloquy, *L'Avare*, I, iv.

revealed. But the soliloquy of comedy is often virtually dialogue still on the same plane as the rest of the play, but addressed to an audience in the front of the house instead of to one on the stage. No solution is attempted in them of the kind of problem with which we are concerned; there is no conflict between content and form, because the form is adequate to the content. The soliloquy of comedy, then, tends to reveal little more than a prompt emotional reaction to events of a kind which can live in public; it may sum up and clarify the deductions and intentions of the character, but only in so far as these may be confidently shared with a complacent group of listeners; it serves not to amplify or deepen the audience's knowledge of the characters' experience, but to ensure that it has the complete and wide-awake grasp of the situation necessary to following the quick movements of the dramatic action.

The attempt to circumvent the technical limitations of drama through the medium of a chorus is, I think, specialized and short-lived; it has seldom recurred in European drama, after the Greek, in any vital manifestation. The soliloquy offers a means far more flexible and far better integrated (at least in appearance) with the body of the dialogue; it has been superseded at times, but seldom universally or for long. One of the most interesting attempts to supersede it has now to be considered, and will, I think, be found to be itself as over-specialized and short-lived as the chorus—the attempt of the strict naturalistic drama to convey all its content, however considerable, without appealing to any non-dramatic resources.

Although, as in the two cases we have already examined, only the dramatic masterpieces will serve to expose the conflict fully, much may here be learnt from plays whose virtue lies in skilful technique. The technique which necessarily follows from the fourth-wall convention demands that the disclosure of what is not spoken be made without any suspense of the strictly naturalistic form and content of the dialogue. Only, therefore, in the plays in which there is profound or complex thought and feeling to be conveyed will there be conflict or resolution. The majority of second-rate plays of this kind proceed very comfortably through their

allotted three, four or five acts without any sign that the
characters are experiencing anything more than they state
(or at least indicate) in their excellently natural dialogue.
But when a master in drama attempts this form we have a
conflict as interesting as any of those we have already
suggested, for the pressure and wealth of his thought inevitably rebel against a type which adds to the inherent
limitations of drama a wholly artificial series of restrictions
arising from the cult of naturalism.

The revelation of unspoken thought within this somewhat
tyrannical scheme is variously attempted by each dramatist
who handles it, sometimes variously from play to play.
Ibsen, who seems to have been largely (though perhaps
unintentionally) responsible for the development of this
phase of drama, never subjected himself completely to its
demands. In each of his social plays, *Pillars of Society*,
A Doll's House, *Ghosts*, *The Enemy of the People*, *The Wild
Duck*, and *Hedda Gabler*, he presents a precise picture of
everyday life in a specific setting, such as might, except for
the concentration and selection in character and event, be
witnessed by someone looking through the walls of a small-
town house and watching the inmates at the crisis of their
fortunes. Through the greater part of most of these plays
he appears to have no resource but the dialogue; certainly
he never suspends its natural movement to make way for
any convention that would allow him to reveal what dialogue
excludes. But much more takes place in his people's minds
than they would speak in this everyday life, and that ' more '
must be communicated to us if the potency and significance
of the action are to be revealed. Ibsen does not break his
way out of the difficulty, but circumvents it by creating a
situation that calls for the elucidation of past conduct and
present positions. Norah speaks out at the moment of
leaving her husband; it was impossible for her to do so
before, yet impossible for her not to do so when challenged.
Mrs. Alving and Manders, similarly challenged by each other
and by circumstance, disentangle the motives of their past
acts upon which rests their present relationship to society.
There is perhaps a flaw in the form of Norah's statement,
inasmuch as her thought seems to have run clearer than is

probable so soon after the experience; but it is a flaw that we do not notice at first or second reading. And even this suspicion is removed in the similar dialogue in *Ghosts*, where Mrs. Alving presents an interpretation of her life that has grown clear through years of stern and lonely reflection. This inner life, these thoughts, these reflections are the main matter of the play; the problem of their presentation is solved by a movement so bold and direct that it cannot be called a device, by making the play serve and lead up to them instead of making their function subsidiary to the action of the play. But a limitation has been circumvented nevertheless. Nor is Ibsen's skill baffled in those plays in which he does not reach his purpose solely by this method. Well within the frame of the drama as yet, but charged with power to illuminate the undercurrents of thought, is the symbolism that appears unobtrusively in *Pillars of Society* and runs clearly through *The Wild Duck*. The symbol of the wild duck acts as a recurring reminder of the mental habits of more than one of the characters and illuminates thereby the hidden selves that Ekdal, Hjalmar, and Gregers all, in their different ways, reject or evade. The dramatic form has been strictly maintained, but a means of circumventing its limitation has, nevertheless, been found. How strict is Ibsen's observance of dramatic form in the social dramas can be seen if we look forward to the first play of a later group, *The Master Builder*. Here the chain of related symbols checks us from time to time, as surely as does a choric ode and more noticeably than a Jacobean soliloquy; in compelling us to look beyond the literal meaning of some of Solness's speeches for that inner life that bewilders even the man himself, it interrupts the effect of verisimilitude; we know that in this play we have passed from the naturalistic drama to another kind. But in the social dramas, up to and even including *Rosmersholm*, Ibsen is strict in his mediation between content and form, even when it is the intransigent form of the fourth-wall drama. The fullness of our knowledge of his people, of the other life stirring below the surface of their lives, is a witness to the skill with which the limitations have been circumvented.

Beside his bold use of the conversation piece and of

symbolism to indicate what cannot find its way into normal
dialogue, Ibsen makes full use of the methods which the form
most clearly invites. No small part of our understanding
comes from the order and tempo of presentation. What we
are told by a given piece of dialogue is what we might suppose
ourselves to overhear in life, but because this is drama and
a selection from life, the order in which we hear these various
passages, their relation to those to which they are in juxtaposition, no less than the implications in the tempo and
setting of each passage, deepen the significance of them all
by cross illumination. We are all aware of this mastery in
the first act of *The Wild Duck*; analysis hardly reveals one
sentence, much less a whole passage, which could be discarded
or transposed without loss to the significance of some other
passage.

The fact that Ibsen shook himself free of this type of drama,
after some five or six plays had explored its potentialities,
is fair warning that it was not fruitful, and in some of his
successors the dangers of subjection to the demands of this
form became clearer. Two English dramatists of some
distinction, Galsworthy and Granville Barker, it is true,
observe its demands with exact fidelity, and one or two other
names could be added to these. The skill with which the
undertones of thought and feeling are conveyed, without
resort to the conventions that break the strict dramatic
presentation, is one of the triumphs of craftsmanship; the
technique of *Strife* is flawless, yet the pressure and significance
of the matter are undeniable. A careful analysis of the
opening passages of this and other plays suggests selection
and manipulation of dialogue, so as to achieve the maximum
of concentration and economy without loss of verisimilitude,
and reminds us of the process revealed by Ibsen's five
successive drafts of the first act of *Pillars of Society*. The
dialogue evolved achieves what all strictly dramatic dialogue
should achieve, it conveys more by the combination of statement, implication and juxtaposition than could a passage of
equal length which had the freedom of direct narrative or
statement.[1] This use is nothing new; Shakespeare's opening

[1] Henry Arthur Jones, a skilful man of the theatre, describes the
position neatly as early as 1903 : ' No man should think himself a

passages often reveal simultaneously the necessary information as to the situation and relations of the chief characters,
the events which have preceded the opening of the play,
something of the characters of the speakers, and the first
movements of the episode which is to start the action within
the play.   But the Elizabethan never attempted to do this
while maintaining strict verisimilitude throughout the action
of the play.   To do this involves a most skilful circumvention
of the double limitations of this peculiar type and, as such,
must be seriously considered in any examination of dramatic
aesthetics.

Nevertheless, this attempt to do away with convention, to
pretend that a play is not a play but a piece of actual life,
makes unnecessary demands upon the technical athleticism
of the playwright, and, with any but great artists, there is a
tendency to over-prize that particular mental agility.   So
excellent is the virtuosity that, as in the rather different case
of the *pièce bien faite*, some fifty years earlier, it may be
accepted in place of content by playwright and critic alike.
But however necessary it may be for a pianist to practise
certain exercises, it is not customary, for all that, to give a
concert consisting of scales.   Moreover, in the continually
increasing effort to remove the last suspicions of dramatic
demeanour from their plays, while yet using the dramatic
form, with its artificial concentration and selection, the
minor followers of Ibsen are liable to overload the play with
devices for avoiding the suspicion of device, thereby choking
the action and slackening the tension.   They do us a considerable service, demonstrating, by the method of *reductio ad
absurdum*, that unwavering fidelity to the probable is as
incompatible with genuine drama on the one hand as a dis-

---

dramatist until he can so condense and inform his dialogue that behind
it is hidden and packed up a narrative of greater volume than the
dialogue itself. . . . Whatever is essential for the audience to learn
must, by suggestion, by implication, by side-lights and contrivances,
be given by the dramatist in dialogue which shall convey all necessary
facts of history, all necessary facts of character, all relations of the
persons in the play to one another and to the main theme—shall do
all this in far fewer words than would be used by a story-teller in giving
the same information in the third person ' (' Literary Critics and the
Drama ', in *The Nineteenth Century Review*, 1903).

regard for the effect of immediacy may be upon the other. Under their guidance we come full circle and admit that the intrusion of an element of non-dramatic expression appears, paradoxically, to render some necessary service to drama. Major drama, except by a superlative effort, which even Ibsen eventually refused, has never been continuously naturalistic in form and content throughout the whole length of a play. Great drama has a habit of retaining the proved and fertile conventions, these being, apparently, essential to its life. To refuse them is but to multiply the devices for concealing devices and to fill the play with technical gymnastics to the destruction of significant content. There is a point in all art at which verisimilitude and reality part company, and this can be observed at work in the technical contortions of the fourth-wall drama as clearly as in any study of the relations between photography and painting.

The final developments of this experiment are interesting, though, I suspect, sterile. There appear to be two main streams in naturalistic drama, and each treats differently this problem of the intractable matter that will not be spoken and yet must be conveyed. The first selects the tendency, characteristic of some phases of modern life, to conceal beneath the surface of behaviour the inner experience and vital preoccupations of the mind. This attempts to solve the technical problem of revealing unspoken thought by making the fact of its suppression the main theme of the play, and calls for a rare and subtle skill to keep us continually aware of its presence. The second selects the equally characteristic tendency to mistrust the adequacy of human judgement in estimating evidence, whether of fact or of motive. This attempts to solve the problem by so constructing the play as to make the conduct of the central character or characters the subject of debate among the others, demonstrating in the course of discussion and experiment the elusiveness of truth and the evasiveness of the hidden, unspoken element in thought. The plays of M. Jean-Jacques Bernard may serve to represent the first and certain of those of Luigi Pirandello the second. Both attack the problem boldly, regarding it as one of human conduct as much as of dramatic technique.

W. B. Yeats, who strongly disliked ' the play of modern manners ', noticed as early as the year 1906 (in his *Discoveries*) that the difficulty of dramatizing the conduct of modern educated people arose from their habit of reticence.   ' When they are deeply moved they look silently into the fire-place.' This convention of behaviour threatened, he believed, the death of serious or tragic drama of present-day life, for the dramatist must make his people unlike themselves if they were to express themselves.   It did not, at that date, occur to him to examine the opposite alternative and consider whether a play could be made out of the very fact that they were inarticulate.   Ibsen solved the problem of unspoken thought in terms of the technique of his own time by making the conversation piece the core of a realistic play, arranging that the situation should force it upon the characters.   M. Jean-Jacques Bernard, in our own day, confronted with the modern tendency to pass over in silence all that is significant and profound in our experience, devised the ' Théâtre de Silence '.[1]   Here everything in the play points towards some essential motive, experience or emotion which is never openly acknowledged.   It is an extremely subtle technique, difficult to practise and not always easy for an audience to follow, but it is a penetrating comment upon the nature and function of the hidden life and unspoken thought of modern civiliza- tion.   It mirrors a world in which what is of deepest signifi- cance is indicated only by implication, and the playwright, contending with almost insuperable difficulties, subdues even this material to dramatic form.   It was, no doubt, as Yeats supposed, this tendency in modern life which devitalized poetic and romantic tragedy, driving it to seek themes remote from the everyday life of its times ; and the necessary aban- donment of a form that was becoming incongruous left the dramatists with the task of conveying the minds of con- ventionally inarticulate beings strictly in terms of what they articulated.   M. Bernard's solution is at once technically brilliant and exquisitely faithful to its material, but again, as in the case of his predecessors, we may wonder whether the cost is not greater than the fruit is worth.

[1] Four plays are well known in England : *L'Ame en Peine, Le Printemps des Autres, Martine, L'Invitation au Voyage.*

The technique of some of Pirandello's plays circumvents the limitation in a slightly different way. Again our interest is skilfully focussed upon a central fact, motive, or prepossession which is never fully defined. We may deduce what we can or strike a balance between the deductions of certain of the characters, but there is again silence at the point of maximum significance. There is no risk of our mistaking the silence for vacancy; everything in the play points towards the central mystery, and in some, such as *Right You Are* and *Naked*, the business of the play arises from the anxiety of the characters to unmask what is concealed. The form is the natural outcome of Pirandello's preoccupation with the relation between consciousness and reality and his perception of the inadequacy of our conscious thought to estimate what is in our unconscious minds. In the greater number of his plays he is concerned with the mystery of personality and the mystery of reality; his interest is therefore primarily in the unspoken thought of which the characters are themselves unconscious rather than in the dramatist's problem of conveying to the audience that of which he and they are conscious and whose expression is inhibited by the conditions of drama. Nevertheless, many of his plays, even *Six Characters in Search of an Author*, throw interesting oblique lights upon the problem, and he delights in playing tricks with our rigid classification of what we are pleased to consider reality.[1] The indication of some essential thought by the negative method of suggestive omission has been used sparingly by dramatists at other times.[2] It is

---

[1] In the long stage direction which follows the mid-act curtain of Act I of *Each In His Own Way*, Pirandello describes the three planes of reality on which the various parts of the play move. ' In the interlude at the end of the second act,' he goes on, ' these three planes of reality will come into contact with one another as the participants in the drama of real life attack the participants in the comedy, the spectators, meantime, trying to interfere. Under such circumstances, it need not be observed, a comedy cannot go on.'

His own comedy is a delicate, ironical comment on this obvious fact, but the words acquire a meaning that is less playful and more critical when we apply them to the brilliant sterile drama of his contemporaries. ' Under such circumstances ', as fourth-wall naturalism has created, drama ' cannot go on '.

[2] Three at least of the Jacobean dramatists—Shakespeare, Middleton, and Ford—can indicate essential thought by what is not said or

the conscious and deliberate use of it in the main theme of
a play which this highly specialized technique has added to
the records of dramatic experiment.

In the twentieth-century revolt against the strict technique
of that fourth-wall drama which immediately preceded it (a
revolt that was already stirring in the late work of Ibsen and
the early work of Strindberg), there is to be found a bewildering succession of experiments with content and form.   The
best of these are notable plays, but perhaps few of them are as
original as they seem at first sight and none more original
than the experimental work of the two great Scandinavians.
Sometimes the dramatists hit out new devices for revealing
the hidden thoughts and passions of their characters, though
often with corresponding loss of that concentration and
immediacy which are the essence of drama.   This restless
eagerness for exploration cannot be disregarded or robbed
of its due credit, but too often it seems to mark only weakness.   The modern reader is sometimes prepared to assume
that these dramatists have something so new to say that they
must consequently find a new dramatic medium or that the
process of expressing old truth in terms of modern social and
psychological conditions itself demands a new technique.
We must not, certainly, exclude this possibility, but we may

---

only partly said. Words well up at intervals, from a mind deeply
engaged with tragic thought or emotion, as asides or irrelevancies in the
midst of the talk that surrounds them, revealing more briefly and more
powerfully even than soliloquy, the path pursued by that mind.   Such
are Lear's speeches (I, v) those of Imogen (*Cymbeline*, I, i) or those of
Beatrice in Middleton's *Changeling* (III, iv).   Ford uses this method in
his own way in *The Broken Heart*, a play whose theme is reticence, ' the
silent griefs that cut the heart-strings ', and in which there are, fittingly,
no soliloquies.   So fine are the overtones of this play and so essential
to our understanding of it that Ford often seems to anticipate the
Théâtre de Silence and share its dangers.   A modern instance may be
found in Strindberg's brief play *The Stronger*; silence is the very means
by which the presence of essential yet unspoken thought is conveyed.
Mr. Sean O'Casey, to come to our own day, turns the resultant dis-
junctive inconsequence of such dialogue to account to image in little
the disintegration of society which is one of the themes of *The Plough
and the Stars* and *The Silver Tassie*.   (See *The Plough and the Stars*, Act I,
pp. 11–12, ed. 1930; a slight dialogue, not tragic but serving the ends
of comic irony.)
   These are but instances taken at random from the drama of the last
three hundred years.

be allowed to suspect that impatience with the traditional demands of dramatic form results more often from failure to achieve supreme artistic control of the material than from any clear and coherent vision of a new form. The problem is still, as always, primarily that of the complete or incomplete subduing of content to form, and this problem is not solved by sacrificing essential parts of either.

We have examined here only one specific, technical problem, though I believe it to be one that goes near the roots and is closely linked with many others. The grouping of modern plays therefore, in relation only to their treatment of this problem, must be, from any other point of view, arbitrary and perhaps unsure. The analysis, moreover, is not helped by the fact that the material is extensive, confused, and brilliant; the variety of its technical devices, even in this field alone, makes the fertility of the Elizabethan invention appear like regimentation and the great traditional form of the Greek or of the Elizabethan appear plain and sober. Unfortunately, this wealth does not imply a corresponding increase in profundity, imagination, or originality. It is related that Innocent III once displayed to St. Dominic the accumulated treasures of the Vatican. ' Thou seest ', he said at the end, ' the time is now past when St. Peter could say, " Silver and gold have I none ".' ' Yes,' replied the saint, ' and the time is also past when he could say to the lame man, " Arise and walk ".'

Several bold and outwardly impressive attempts have been made to reveal unspoken thought by a frank breach with naturalism and the use of some device for interspersing it throughout the normal dialogue.[1] This is not an extension of or a derivative from soliloquy, for there is no attempt to gloss over the contrast or to pretend that both are normal speech : the effect of continuous dramatic form is sacrificed, and we move abruptly from one level of immediacy and probability to another. A thorough exploration of this method was made by Eugene O'Neill in *Strange Interlude* and

[1] In some cases, such as *Strange Interlude*, the distinction between normal speech and that which conveys unspoken thought must be made by the actor's changes of voice and by the freezing of the action on the stage during the lines which the other characters in the play are not supposed to hear.

I

Days Without End and Elmer Rice had used a similar device in parts of *The Adding Machine*.[1] O'Neill's *Strange Interlude* attempts to convey something like the whole of the conscious thought of the characters by sifting in and out of the normal dialogue passages in which we hear what they are thinking but deliberately refraining from speaking. Some admirable contrasts can be made, much light can be thrown on the relation between the speaker's inner thought or emotion and his public utterance, and some additional point is given to those speeches which do not need the accompaniment of a contradictory or amplifying undertone. But the action is unbearably delayed by this attempt to combine the privileges of dramatist and novelist. In *Days Without End* O'Neill confined this double revelation to one character and separated him into two warring personalities, both of whose speeches were heard by the other characters though only one of his figures was visible to them. This was little more than an emphasis on the conflict of Jekyll and Hyde within the man, though, when his two halves were alone together on the stage, a neat medieval device for indicating inner conflict was recalled.

A further step in the same direction is taken by certain plays which include not only a fuller expression of the unspoken conscious thought, but also some expression of the unformulated subconscious thought. Monologue or soliloquy is generally used for this purpose,[2] but it is such soliloquy as the Elizabethans would not have ventured except when madness gave the excuse for the upwelling of uncensored thought normally hidden from the man himself. Different levels of consciousness interact in this way through Eliot's drama of *Sweeney Agonistes*, and O'Casey's *Within the Gates*, while in the second act of *The Silver Tassie* a kind of mass subconsciousness expresses itself directly in the choruses.[3]

In some modern experiments there is a conscious attempt

[1] *The Adding Machine* (1923), Scene II.
[2] As in *The Adding Machine*, I and IV.
[3] The same device becomes little more than a trick, and not a really fruitful one, in Auden and Isherwood's *Dog Beneath the Skin* and *F. 6*, but it comes very near justifying itself in the choric portions of Mr. Eliot's *Family Reunion*, where a fine artist again turns the technicians' invention to significant use.

to use one of the subsidiary arts of the theatre to illuminate
the thought and emotion of the characters. This, like many
other experiments, is an extension of something that can be
found in germ in other plays of all kinds and periods, but the
conscious emphasis now laid upon it carries it into the
category of deliberate experiment. The mood, tone, or
atmosphere that envelops a play has often been indicated
by the poet's own choice of setting; Tourneur's charnel
house, Webster's echoing walls are early imaginative indications of setting that are on the border of symbolism, enhancing the fear or horror of the characters, and at the same time
deepening our sympathy with and apprehension of their
experience. The forest near Athens, the forest of Arden, the
heath near Forres have a similar function. But in all these
the indications are general; they are not symbols of some
specific thought or preoccupation for the revelation of which
we depend largely upon them. To find the equivalent of that
in the Elizabethans we must turn to the ' air-drawn dagger '
or the ghost of Banquo, momentary appearances, not the
continuous setting (even though imaginary) of a whole scene.[1]
When, however, we turn to such a play as O'Neill's *Emperor
Jones* in our own day, we find that the successive settings
of the forest scenes present specific images of the central
character's fears and obsessions as well as indicating the
affinity between his dominant mood and that of the forest
that destroys him. The nightmare scenes are projections of
his own haunted visions, mingling with or substituting themselves for the actual scenery. Whenever, therefore, he is alone
on the stage, the audience sees what he sees, not what a
detached spectator would see—not the heath near Forres, but
the air-drawn dagger. His soliloquies are a running accompaniment to these scenes, but an essential part of the work
of revelation is done by this visual presentation of his terror.
In this and in all similar uses of setting, we see not merely
an actual scene which is in harmony with the character's
mood, but instead, or simultaneously, something which exists
only in his mind. And this visual image, kept before the

[1] The freedom of the Elizabethan dramatist was greater than that
of the modern in that the heath near Forres and the apparitions were
alike present only in the imaginations of the audience.

mind of the audience by use of a particular, subsidiary art of the modern theatre, serves both to illuminate the dialogue and to reveal certain aspects of his thought or experience which the dialogue does not convey. O'Neill's *Emperor Jones* belongs to a rare kind, but there is a less consistent, a partial use of setting to symbolize the contents of the mind which is far more common. It may be traced in the masks and settings of another play of his, *Lazarus Laughed*, in Sean O'Casey's *Within the Gates*, in several of Lenormand's and, typically, in the scene in Rice's *The Adding Machine*, in which the walls of the cashier's bedroom are papered with long columns of manuscript figures.

It has been possible in this last section to suggest only a few of the ways in which modern devices attempt to circumvent this problem. We have, moreover, omitted those experiments which solve the problem by throwing it overboard, whether by transferring the action to a dream world or by reverting to the devices of the medieval morality play. Two of them may be briefly indicated.

One is the relatively large group of twentieth-century plays which transfer the action or a portion of it to a world which is virtually fairy-land.[1] There is free play in that domain for comment and self-revelation that would be impossible to compass plausibly in dialogue in a normal setting. But one of the essential conditions of drama, the revelation of human nature as we are able to study it in the known circumstances of life, has been evaded. Scenes in which the chief characters appear after death, either in an imagined other world or as spirits returning to this world, generally have self-discovery or re-valuation as their purpose, but the revelation is achieved only by virtually destroying character. What is presented is not a man in normal or even abnormal circumstances, but a non-human entity. In that large freedom the laws of drama are relaxed; no reconciliation of content and form is called for when the

[1] Among the most interesting of these are Molnar's *Liliom*, Mr. Coward's *Post Mortem* and Schlumberger's *Miracle at Verdun*. Mr. Shaw's use of this device in the scene in hell in *Man and Superman* is actually a satirical conversation piece cast in the form of a dream and does not, I think, claim to be on the same level of actuality as the rest of the play—though it may contain more significant truth.

central experience, upon which content and action rest, is one that can be expressed only by symbol, fantasy or conjecture.

Those plays, again, which present processes of mind in isolation, divorced from event or from character, are still further from genuine drama and must be regarded as a kind of allegory which has borrowed its outward form. Just as the medieval moralities and moral interludes (*Everyman*, the *Castell of Perseverance*, *Mundus et Infans*) analyse the mind into component parts and attempt to make of these abstractions the agents of the action, so, from a somewhat different psychological starting point, do their modern equivalents, *The Theatre of the Soul*, *The Dream Play*, *The Dance of Death*, *Masses and Man*, *A Bride for the Unicorn*, *Six Characters*,[1] and others too numerous to list. Sometimes, as in the medieval morality, there is a residuum of individual character, the equivalent of a Hickskorner or Everyman, around and about whom the abstractions projected from him contend; or a few individuals (as in *Within the Gates*) are surrounded by figures that, in varying degrees, are rather types or symbols than characters. These make no serious attempt upon the problem of revealing underlying thought within the dramatic form, because there is no longer any distinction between spoken and unspoken thought. When the whole of the action takes place within the ' theatre of the soul ' there will be nothing that we recognize as action springing from character in the actual theatre. The matter of the play is largely unconscious thought, imaged in various ways. Such plays reveal no more distinction between what is commonly spoken and what is commonly suppressed than do the pages of a psycho-analyst's case-books. The presentation of character, upon which drama rests, is here abandoned in favour of symbols.

This chapter has not attempted to survey the history of this peculiar technical problem, but only to indicate what is its nature, in how many and various ways it has been met by

---

[1] By Evreinoff, Strindberg (2), Toller, Denis Johnstone, and Pirandello. To these might be added Capek's drama, known in English as *The Insect Play*.

dramatists, and how unintermittent has been their effort (conscious or unconscious) to overcome one of the most serious technical limitations of the dramatic form.

The problem is, as we have noticed, only one of many similar conflicts of a technical kind, but in considering it we realize afresh the vital relation between convention and great drama. There is a continual struggle to maintain such effect of actuality as is necessary for conviction, upon the one hand, and to convey to the audience, on the other, more knowledge of the issues of the play than strict verisimilitude will allow. It is at this point that conventions, tacitly agreed upon between audience and author and varying from age to age, are discovered to be not a hindrance but an aid to the finest dramatic achievement. To trace the nature and effectiveness of some of the conventions that have been attempted has been the task of this chapter.

The function of these conventions resembles in some degree that of imagery in drama. Like imagery they attempt to overcome the inherent limitations of drama and extend its scope without making with the demands of dramatic form a breach open enough to damage illusion in the theatre. That they do not accomplish this so unostentatiously as does imagery is evident from the superficial examination we have made. But their processes are alike in that both proceed by circumvention and do not as a rule lead to those conflicts on a major scale that we considered in some earlier chapters.

CHAPTER SEVEN

THE EQUILIBRIUM OF TRAGEDY

FINALLY, we may consider one more aspect of the function of limitation in drama.

There is, as we briefly suggested in the foregoing studies, a constant and creative conflict between content and form, technique and medium. But of no less significance is a conflict arising from limitation of mood. And the equilibrium which here results is essential to the highest reach of dramatic art. Indeed, in considering it we may perceive certain of the basic relations between limitation and achievement in drama. It is seen most clearly in tragedy, for tragedy depends most intimately upon the preservation of a strict and limiting balance between two contrary readings of life and their sequent emotions at work within the poet's mind. Such equilibrium is thus the distinguishing mark of the highest achievement in this kind, individual works tending to approach supremacy in so far as they derive from this conflict and reveal this resultant balance.

Other characteristics of fine tragedy must of course be present also if this is to be achieved in any play. There must be strength of emotion revealed through character and through significant related actions and underlying thought which further relates passion and event. Again, as in all great drama, directness, rapidity, and shapeliness of presentation must serve the ends simultaneously of concentration and of probability, and the resulting beauty of passion, form, and thought will constitute dramatic poetry, whether the vehicle be prose or verse. Finally, this image of tragic circumstance which we call a tragedy must involve catastrophe, either material or spiritual, arising naturally from the action and forming an integral part of it.

A rough description such as this allows us to reject, without further examination, certain types of play which bear a superficial or a partial resemblance to great tragedy. Melodrama fails to integrate passion and event by thought, fails sometimes to relate the catastrophe to the action, and lacks in general that depth of imagination upon which the revelation of character and emotion depend; again, a mere chronicle of evil or of pathetic event, even though shapely, may fail to satisfy our sense of tragedy from lack of intensity in passion and in thought; and a play in which death or destruction comes by accident will fail again, however finely imagined, because the catastrophe is not integral to the play and to its underlying thought.[1]

But in great tragedy there is an element common to the individual plays, though differing in form and theme, an element which marks both the treatment of the material and the nature of the resulting interpretation : it is the presence of that conflict, to which we have just referred, between two impressions made by his experience upon the poet's mind.

The part of this experience which is most clearly revealed is the intense awareness of evil and pain. But in conflict with this specific response to fact and event is another of a wholly different kind; the intuitive and often undefined apprehension ·of another universe implying other values. Beyond the realization of evil and pain (and the work of art will be great in proportion as this is profound), beyond the apprehension of an alien destiny that appears to shape man's action, there is the perception, at once more comprehensive and less explicit, of a possible resolution, of some reconciliation with or interpretation in terms of good.   The impressions in conflict may be of various kinds; of a malevolent and a beneficent world-order; of apparent lawlessness against underlying law, a casual against a causal, a chaotic against a patterned universe.   And the unresolved conflict between them will at first give rise to a sense of mystery; to the assumption that evil can never be sounded, however thoroughly it be analysed, that its causes will never fully reveal themselves, even to the most passionate questioning.

It is here that, in the finest tragic writing, there is equilibrium.   The reality of evil and pain is not denied; if it

_____

[1] These are instances only of the types of play which fall short of the category of tragedy. Any reader of drama will readily think of many others.

were, tragedy would not speak to man's condition as it has done from the time of Aeschylus to the present day. Nevertheless, something is revealed which makes possible the transvaluation of the values upon which this rests; the works of art which we call tragedies are distinguished from others, not only by technical characteristics of subject-matter or form, but also by the balance maintained between conflicting readings of the universe and of man's condition and destiny. The supreme works in this kind reveal that balance in the highest degree, thus satisfying most nearly man's need to find his complex and contradictory experience transmuted unto the enduring form of art. Certain tragedies, it is true, fail to maintain complete balance, some lessening their hold on the imagination by presenting irremediable evil and a satanic universe, and some, with similar consequences, indicating remedies so immediate or so easily defined that men's judgement and innate sanity mistrust them. Both kinds may nevertheless remain within the category of tragedy, provided they do not destroy either of the elements in whose conflict the average man recognizes an essential part of his own dual experience.

The characteristic balance thus obtained results, as we have said, in a play of a certain quality. In content and in thought tragedy is, like all great art, an interpretation of some part of the universe of man's experience, but inasmuch as it is dramatic it is primarily an interpretation by implication, by the emphasis it lays on certain parts of that experience, the significance with which it invests them, rather than by explicit or direct commentary. The part of this experience which it selects involves suffering and some kind of catastrophe, and these significant of something more than the bare facts actually present. Balance is thus maintained in all great tragedy; suffering and catastrophe upon the one hand and upon the other a relation (often unspecified and undefined) with some fundamental or universal law whose operation justifies or compensates them. From this arises the conflict of impressions; evident evil against partially hidden yet immanent and overruling good. Thus far all tragedy is akin.

In what writers is this most fully and most clearly revealed ? In none perhaps more than in some of the major works of

Aeschylus, Sophocles, Shakespeare, and Ibsen. Here, though the evidence of pain and evil is never denied, the final position is not despair or rebellion, but a perception of that in man's destiny which resolves pain in exultation. (It may rise at times to a willing collaboration with the purposes of the unrevealed powers whose presence is felt though never fully understood.) Some such balance as this is to be found in the work of most of the world's greatest tragic writers and we may observe not only its nature but the various means by which that nature is maintained. In certain types of formally archaic tragedy the outer action or story may indicate the reading of life derived from the evidence of evil in fact and event, while that other universe and its differing values may, as in the Aeschylean chorus, be presented directly as comment. In another type, while the outer action may still present that first reading, the second may depend upon an inner action proceeding independently, though in close relation with the outer, and consisting of the experience of individual minds exploring the world of thought or of imagination. Shakespeare's major tragedies and such of his contemporaries' as achieve tragic balance seem generally to be of this kind. In a third kind again, where there is little or no comment and yet no clearly distinguished inner action, the implications of form alone maintain the balance. This appears to be the nature of the equilibrium in certain of the plays of Sophocles.

Some of the tragedies of Aeschylus present the two balancing perceptions—which by their balance make the tragic mood—in different and separate mediums.[1] To the action or story, which is the main part of the play, falls the presentation of evil and that measure of implicit comment, through emphasis and selection, which is inseparable from creative art. It is left to the choruses to make the explicit comment on the action which subordinates it to the surrounding universe of order and law whose significance would else be obscure. The balance is superbly achieved and main-

[1] And with this method we may associate all subsequent imitations of the Greek choric method, the many plays in which a virtually choric function is forced upon certain characters and one or two modern variations which will be noticed later.

tained, but by a division of functions, the one reading of life being presented by strictly dramatic, the other by non-dramatic methods. The theme of the *Agamemnon* and the *Choephori* is the implacable evil of the responsibility for sin, but throughout the plays, as through most of Shakespeare's, there are seemingly contradictory references to forms of good apparently outside the evil; Zeus is all-wise, all-powerful, the ' Saviour ', he who pities.[1] But, unlike Shakespeare or any but a few other tragic dramatists, Aeschylus comments not only on the fact but on the relationship between the two balancing forces. Without reducing the significance of suffering or of evil, and while yet maintaining the equilibrium between it and the enveloping beneficence of Zeus, Aeschylus reveals the process by which the two are linked. Zeus does not merely pity, but leads man through pain to wisdom, so that the very suffering which arose from the presence of evil becomes the means of conversion and beatitude. Zeus himself became the all-comprehending by no other road.

In the two strict tragedies, the *Agamemnon* and the *Choephori*, there is little more than this indication of the relation between the two and the tragic balance is maintained. In the third play, when the Erinyes become the Eumenides, we pass from the drama of tragic equilibrium to that drama of beatitude which has been described in an earlier chapter,[2] and the process is elucidated in Aeschylus's picture of the reconciliation of the two forces.

This method is not peculiar to the Greek drama of the fifth century B.C. Though it involves an interruption of the strict dramatic effect, it falls completely out of use only when naturalism has a fictitious value, as in the fourth-wall drama of the late nineteenth and early twentieth centuries in Europe. It will obviously be found in all imitations of or derivations from Greek drama at any period and in that breaking in of narrative method which appears to be natural to some drama, such as that of medieval Europe, In the early

---

[1] *Choephori*, 639 45. Aeschylus uses the chorus for these references; certain of the Elizabethans assign a temporary choric function to characters within the action; Shakespeare always uses the pure dramatic method and his commentary or references come only from those characters whose nature it is to speak them.

[2] Chapter II.

phases of its development. Modern variations may relate
to either or both of these forerunners. Goethe, in the first
part of *Faust*, assigned to his choric and prologue figures part
at least of the function of redressing the tragic balance, and
other kinds of extra-dramatic commentary are used for
kindred purposes to the present day (as in Drinkwater's
Abraham Lincoln). Plays, again, which, with varying
degrees of plausibility, temporarily invest certain of the
characters from the main action with choric functions
virtually use the same method. For so long as the choric
commentary lasts (though it be only for a line or two) for so
long the two balancing interpretations are presented in
different and separate mediums. Many of the Elizabethans
used this method, briefly and abstemiously, with fine effect :
Webster had peculiar skill in this. And in much of the
tragedy written in Europe during the last thirty years—to
jump the intervening years with their many interesting uses,
especially in Germany—the tendencies to expressionism on
the one hand and to symbolism on the other have alike
tempted playwrights to the same device, which they handle
with confidence and fluency, but with somewhat less than
Webster's effectiveness.

The balance between manifest evil and immanent good is
maintained by a widely different process in the work of
Shakespeare and most of his contemporaries. Except for a
few extra-dramatic conventions irrelevant to the present
issue, these plays are wholly dramatic in form, and such
comment as there is is necessarily implicit. But here an
outer and an inner action can be distinguished clearly;
the outer, like the action of the *Oresteia*, presents by its story
the reading of life which observes and admits the nature of
evil and of suffering; again, as in Aeschylus's play, with
that element of implicit comment which is inseparable from
emphasis and selection. But behind this, coextensive with
and yet frequently independent of it, is action on another
plane of being which we may regard as an inner action, made
up of the experiences of the minds, the thought-life of the
characters.[1] Though the distinction between the two does

[1] This has already been described in the discussion of *Samson
Agonistes* (Chapter II).

not become so marked in drama as to force itself upon the reader's observation until perhaps the middle of the nineteenth century,[1] it is already visible in that of Shakespeare, and it is upon this inner action that the function devolves of maintaining tragic equilibrium by counterpoising the presentation of evil in the outer action. The thought-world of Cordelia or of Kent has relatively little effect upon the course of those events in *Lear* that are shaped by and shape the other characters; but it is of immense effect in our final impression of the universe revealed by the play, reaching its triumph in certain passages that, looking through death, create the harmony of the play.

To some degree already in Shakespeare, as in all major dramatists, a third means of balance is disclosed, and in a few, of a rare quality, it appears to be the only means and to work alone. Perhaps the earliest instances of this last kind are to be found in some of the plays of Sophocles,[2] where the interpretative function of the choric odes is less than in those of Aeschylus; here the balance is achieved within the strictly dramatic part of the play, yet without the help of any discernible separate inner action. The presence of a beneficent world-order, of immanent good, is implied in such plays as *Oedipus* or *Macbeth* by the presence of form [3] as an integral part of the work of art even when evil or suffering is the theme. The impression left upon the mind is of an equilibrium between the manifestation of evil and the embodiment of the principle of order. Beauty of form and expression then represent by implication the forces of righteousness and beneficence of which Aeschylus speaks directly in the choric odes. In plays of this group, harmony

[1] But to this group belongs a great part of the tragic work of Shakespeare, Lessing, Schiller, Hebbel, Ibsen, and such widely differing moderns as, to choose a few names at random, Galsworthy, Synge, and Hauptmann.

[2] It is hard to find any other dramatist except Tcheckov in whom the tragic balance appears to depend entirely upon this, though it is a contributory factor to that balance in the work of nearly all great dramatists.

[3] The functions of imagery which have already been indicated (Chapter V above) and those of prosody contribute to this effect. But the significance of form is more than the effect of the specific formal details.

of form is achieved despite the inherent evil or hideousness
of the theme, and so profound is the transmutation that it
becomes an image of that reconciliation by which order and
beauty convert all things into themselves, by which the
Erinyes become the Eumenides and we pass from an *Inferno*
to a *Paradiso*.

We have already noticed [1] that on either side of this central
group, in which the equilibrium of tragedy is thus maintained, there are to be found other types of great tragic
drama in which the balance is threatened by a greater
emphasis upon the positive or the negative interpretation,
by the acceptance in the poet's mind primarily of the latent
or potential good or of the manifest evil. Poets who differ
as widely as Milton and Ibsen may be found in the first group
and those as far apart as Euripides, Marlowe, and Strindberg
in the second.

In Milton's *Samson Agonistes* we found a peculiarly clear
instance of that overbalancing in the direction of positive
interpretation which is inseparable from religious drama and
renders its strict form incompatible with tragedy. What
was there said of Milton may be said, with certain modifications in detail, of Calderon at one extreme and of certain
modern plays at the other.[2] But not all the plays that overset the balance on the positive side are religious drama, nor
is the dissolution of the tragic mood always effected by a
progression into beatitude. The last hundred years have
produced notable groups of plays which lay so strong an
emphasis upon the remediable nature of evil and indicate so
strong a confidence in the near or immediate removal of
suffering by the modification of social conditions that they
cease to be tragedy as surely, though by a different road, as
does religious drama. Ibsen, whose social problem plays are
largely responsible for the growth of this kind, seldom wrote
plays of even technically tragic form while his belief in this

[1] Chapter II.
[2] We may instance among the moderns (taking as wide a range as
possible) Yeats' *Countess Cathleen*, Lunacharski's *Faust and the City*,
and Mr. O'Neill's *Lazarus Laughed*. These have the technical form of
tragedy, but it is clear that they are drawn away from true tragic
balance by the overpowering strength of the positive interpretation,
whether this last is explicit or implicit.

social amelioration was at its height.[1] But the heritage
passes to his successors, Hauptmann and Toller in Germany,
Galsworthy in England, Odets in America, and a host of
others in both continents.

Characteristic of certain of their tragedies, though not of
all in equal degree, is the temporal nature of the suffering.
Though not as a rule accidental or insufficiently related to
action or to theme, it yet does not move us as does suffering
whose cause is in part at least inexplicable. For in each of
these plays a remedy is known or can be guessed at. In
The Weavers, *The Machine Wreckers*,[2] *The Silver Box*,
Justice; in many of the plays of Brieux; even in the work
of Elizabeth Baker, Stanley Houghton, and Granville Barker,
social readjustments not utterly beyond human might would
resolve most of the evil that causes the suffering and so leads
to catastrophe, material or spiritual.[3] In its extreme form
such drama shades into the propaganda play, which lies
outside the scope of this study,[4] where the remedy is specific
and the case immediate; Clifford Odets' *Waiting for Lefty*
leaves no impression of pity or bewilderment, but focusses
the mind by indignation and wrath upon the remedy. This
so lessens the significance of pain, through offering the
assurance of a cure, that the play falls out of harmony even
with man's cruder impression of the fundamental nature of
evil. As Toller himself pointed out, there is a clear distinction to be drawn between the drama which is primarily
social propaganda and that which is in reality tragic : ' For

[1] Already in *Ghosts* and certainly in *The Wild Duck* there is the
implication that no mere social adjustment will eliminate the causes of
suffering, for these are too deeply rooted in man's nature to be reached
from without.

[2] It is perhaps only in these two plays that Hauptmann and Toller
imply clearly that a remediable maladjustment is the main cause of
the suffering and sin. In general their tragedy is more nearly balanced
and implies clearly that the continuance of evil has in it an element of
mystery akin to man's nature itself.

[3] In certain of the later of these plays there is a tendency to combine
spiritual catastrophe with material or to substitute it for it, while
nevertheless implying that some at least of the causes are remediable.
Such a combination is certainly ' enough to make it no tragedy '.

[4] Even when it has the superficial form of tragedy, the true propaganda play seldom maintains strict dramatic technique. It tends to
revert to thinly disguised exposition. This may have many virtues
but they are not those of drama.

only unnecessary suffering can be vanquished, the suffering which arises out of the unreason of humanity, out of an inadequate social system. There must always remain a residue of suffering, the lonely suffering imposed upon mankind by life and death. And only this residue is necessary and inevitable, is the tragic element of life and of life's symbolizer, art.' [1]

The mood of this social drama, then, even when it assumes the technical form of tragedy, is not in essence tragic, for the evil arises precisely out of this ' inadequate social system ', and more significant than the material chosen is the emphasis and orientation given to it. Any given play of this group, that is to say, might have been written in the tragic mood if the light had been focussed, not upon a defect in the machinery of justice (which is adjustable), but upon that streak of innate injustice in man's nature which is far less accessible, which would express itself no doubt in some other form if not in this. It is worth observing in this connexion that the latter half of Ibsen's own career reveals a steady progression from the non-tragic to the tragic emphasis, from the examination of evil in its more readily remediable forms to the exploration of deeper and deeper-lying evil and, finally, to that which baffles prescription. As we pass from the *Pillars of Society* to *The Wild Duck*, we reach the borders of central, balanced tragedy and with Rosmer and Borkman we enter the world of Orestes and Hamlet. For all its earnestness, this social drama rests, in fact, upon a more superficial reading of life than tragedy ' of the centre ', and in this it contrasts sharply with religious drama of which the finest kinds seek out and resolve the potent and seemingly ineradicable forms of evil. It is not without significance that few great dramatists have touched it or continued long to write it; most of them pass on to the profounder forms of meditative tragedy or to that drama which, as we have already suggested, passes beyond tragedy itself.

There are plays, on the other hand, that derive primarily from a negative or destructive reading of life, and these also

[1] The quotation here is from the author's Introduction to the English Translation of *Seven Plays* (1934), but the same distinction is drawn in the *Letters* and is implied in *Masses and Man*.

serve to define the limitations of strict tragedy and to reveal the ease with which its balance can be destroyed by disregarding their boundaries. Here also deviations from the centre may be of two kinds, approximately equivalent to the two we have just traced. Just as the constructive thinker may destroy tragic balance by the assurance either of religious revaluation or of social readjustment, so the playwright of the opposite kind may destroy it by the assumption of a spiritually evil world-order or of an irremediable mechanism or chaos. The first approximates to Satanism, the second to pessimistic materialism; both destroy the balance in ways opposite and parallel to those we have just examined. The first, the Satanists, are necessarily among the rarest tragic writers, for their interpretation involves, not the mere observation of evil phenomena, but the assumption of a system. More common are the writers of the second group (to be set over against the social reformers), who view event and transcribe it with quiet or with savage despair and admit neither qualifying evidence nor hope.

A large part of the social-problem drama of our day, that part which is critical without being constructive, may be of this later kind : when, in addition, the form is that of tragedy, we find such plays as Strindberg's *Miss Julia* or *The Father*, Granville Barker's *Waste*, George Kaiser's *From Morn to Midnight*, the Capeks' *The Insect Play*, Elmer Rice's *The Adding Machine*, and Lenormand's *L'Homme et ses Fantômes*. Few of these plays are great tragedy and, as we suggested in speaking of the social-problem play of the preceding category, few can fairly be named with that tragedy of the centre which we took as our point of departure. And this follows naturally from the relaxing of that tension imposed by the inherent limitations of the tragic mood : except in the rare instances of the religious drama or of its anti-type, the Satanic drama, it is seldom that a play which for any reason evades this law of balance has greatness of passion and of thought. Many of them prove, however, of great interest in analysis, revealing clearly the destruction of balance by negation.

Such plays reveal a clear conception of misery, which they usually study (like their anti-type of the previous group) in terms of one, precisely-drawn social organization, though

K

they too sometimes attempt to give this universality. Their theatre technique is often brilliant and nothing, in situation or emotion, seems forced or pretentious; such work may well be too savage and too honest for staginess. Even when a modern reader has allowed for the disturbance of his judgement by the immediacy of a contemporary theme, he may still see much that would grip the imagination of a generation that came to the play knowing nothing of those immediate conditions. In many of these plays the resources of episode, dialogue, setting, and theatre device are used with bare economy and striking effect, to show the imprisonment of the human soul in circumstance. We watch a vicious circle contract like the curves of a helical spring; the surroundings limit the experience, the experience limits the power of reason and imagination, and the maimed imagination then in turn avoids such experience as change of circumstance might allow. Nevertheless, we are conscious that what we have before us falls short in some way of tragedy. The presentation of evil and of suffering may be as implacable as the writer's strength can make it, but we are left with the disturbing conviction that what we have witnessed is an incomplete reading of life.

This theme and this treatment may be found in the characteristic play of the theatre at one extreme or in the reflective play of psychological analysis at the other, in plays as widely severed as Rice's *The Adding Machine* [1] and Lenor-

---

[1] At the risk of becoming unnecessarily explicit we might examine this, a highly representative play of its kind. It is a study of the inarticulate and uncomprehending death-agonies of a human spirit imprisoned in the mean monotony and vulgar pretensions of present-day black-coat slavery. After the earlier scenes, of mingled naturalism and symbolism, have laid before us the process of this fate, there follows a group of scenes in a world beyond death whose analytic technique and freer tempo allow the author to generalize the experiences of the earlier acts in an implicit commentary upon the misusing of the soul's capacity for life. There is no alleviation, poetic or comic; the only variations in the play are the skilful changes of tension. Life, through a succession of reincarnations, is controlled by a vast adding machine progressing rhythmically to a foreknown result. This mechanism, which cannot be called a world-order, for the inference is not clearly enough drawn in the play, tends only to evil and to destruction of spirit. There is no suggestion of surrounding law, but only of the self-contained laws by which the soul's downward and negative progression is determined—just as are the totals of the adding machine. There is no attempt to

mand's *Simoun*. The unquestioned assumption that suffering is the work of a malevolent machine does not satisfy our understanding, for it no more fits the whole of our experience than does Clifford Odets' opposite and parallel assumption that the evil of the world is remediable by a change of social organization. The interpretation in terms of a limited mechanistic scheme involves no equilibrium, for the play does not lead the mind outward towards a wider emotional and speculative affirmation; it imprisons it instead in a limited area of pain. Such plays place themselves outside the category of tragedy because, by laying the whole emphasis upon evil and suffering, they destroy all balance. And this is true of a large number of modern plays that haunt us by their simultaneous force and restraint, bringing home to our imaginations their themes of misery, grief, defeat, and injustice. Nevertheless we refuse to call them tragedy because they do not square with the whole of our experience.

Finally, there is the rare negative form which might be called Satanic tragedy, the drama which oversets tragic balance, not merely by denying immanent good, but by implying a Satanic universe, a world-order behind the manifestation of event as evil as the event itself. To this kind belong among others, some of the plays of Euripides, Marlowe's *Faustus*, some of Strindberg; among the more recent writers Lenormand sometimes approaches it.[1] This group of plays contrasts sharply with the two we have just considered, in that, at its height, magnitude of theme and power of passion again appear as distinguishing characteristics. This was true also of its direct opposite, religious drama,[2] for there also some attempt at interpretation of

---

throw light upon this from any other direction; nothing conflicts with the impression of pain and evil because there are no other forces, except in the too easily stifled imagination of the central figure, the victim.

[1] The vision of an evil world-order in *Medea* and *The Troades* appears consistent enough to justify regarding them as Satanic drama. Strindberg at his most coherent and forcible makes a similar reading of life (in *Miss Julia* and *The Father*), while Lenormand, slender as is his contribution in general, approaches it in *A L'Ombre du Mal*.

[2] Provided always that we continue to restrict that term to the drama of religious experience and do not extend it to include all drama written in terms of given theological assumptions.

L

life formed a background of thought and found its way directly or indirectly into the total effect even of the outer action. But in the drama of Satanism not only is there a more or less clearly implied interpretation of the universe surrounding the events, but, by reason of its conflict with the systems of positive religion, this interpretation will generally be original to the writer. Thus, in the major Satanic drama there is presupposed a mind both comprehensive and original, strong and wide enough in scope to synthesize disparate material into an organic system and with an individualism tenacious enough to withstand the imaginative force of prevailing assumptions. Nevertheless, even the plays of this group disturb, in greater or less degree, that supreme balance which characterizes tragedy ' of the centre '. Though in less degree than the other negative plays, those of materialistic pessimism, they fall short by presenting a universe—even though patterned and not chaotic—which corresponds but imperfectly with the dual, if contradictory, experience of man.

The peculiar Satanic negation appears in different ways in the plays of Euripides and of Marlowe. Euripides uses the facilities of the Greek chorus to comment upon a universe controlled now by an evil world-order and now by mixture of casualty and cause, while Marlowe, in *Dr. Faustus*, uses the more consistently dramatic Jacobean form to present a steadfast picture of an evil world-order on which there is no comment except by implication.

Euripides, through the familiar imagery of the old gods, reveals the irresponsible, meaningless or even malevolent forces that overbear man's valour. His gods, it is true, are more powerful than man, but certain of them are less noble, and from them comes the frustration which annuls creation, confuses valour, and cripples wisdom.[1]

Even in those plays where this interpretation is less clearly defined, the perception of pain and the poet's sympathy with it outweigh all else. And Euripides' nearest approach to a vindication of life's processes would appear to be Hecuba's

---

[1] Some at least of the repetitions of this passage must be presumed to be Euripides' intention. (*Medea* 1415–19, *Alcestis*, 1159–63, *Helen*, 1688–92, *Bacchae*, 1388–92, *Andromache*, 1284–48.)

in *The Troades*, where she justifies the sufferings of Troy as the raw material of art.[1]

Marlowe, whose tragedy appears at its height and in characteristic form in *Faustus*, takes up a unique position as a tragic thinker, because of the implacable paradox on which his reading of the universe rests; man's innate fallibility on the one hand, and, on the other, the infallibility demanded by inflexible law.[2] To this paradox there is only one conclusion : " Why then belike we must sin and so consequently die."   The precision and finality of this deduction indicate a vision terrifying alike in its assumptions and in its omissions.   For implicit in Marlowe's premiss is the predestination of man to destruction by some determinate power capable of purpose and intention, and, as such purpose can only be sadistic, the world order it implies must derive from a Satanism more nearly absolute than that of Euripides.[3]

But neither in this play nor elsewhere does Marlowe state this assumption in explicit terms and the implication itself rests on a few passages in *Faustus*.[4] Even there it is rather by silence and omission that he reveals his belief that evil is not only inherent in man's destiny but both irremediable and predetermined.   Only a consistent vision of a Satanic universe could beget the initial paradox ; never does Marlowe raise the question : Why, if the laws of the universe be such, should man, himself a part of that universe, be so irreconcileably opposed to them ?   To a convinced Satanist it is, in fact, no paradox.   Given a sadistic and malevolent power directing the world-order there is no inducement to postulate a further transcendent power or intelligence, relating or

---

[1] *Troades*, 1240–45.   Just so Deirdre, in the Cuchulainn cycle and in Synge's play, thinks of her sorrow as a song ' that shall be sung for ever '.

Both these passages put briefly and explicitly an estimate of the function of art in which is implicit the conclusion drawn a few pages earlier in discussing the relation of form to tragic balance in the Sophoclean tragedy.

[2] Like Fulke Greville after him, Marlowe, in the opening argument of the play, sees the

> Wearisome condition of humanity,
> Born under one law, to another bound.

[3] More nearly indeed, than that of any dramatist known to me.

[4] Principally I, i, I, iii, II, ii, V, i and ii.   (The references are to Boas's edition.)

reconciling the contradictions of man's capacity and God's demands. And so Marlowe achieves, not a balance between two interpretations of the universe, but immobility and rigidity of protest. In his drama the spirit of man is set against the universe, but there is no equilibrium between two worlds of thought. For Marlowe, at the time of *Faustus*, did not question the nature of the world-order. He saw it steadily and saw it evil.

So complete does Marlowe's Satanism seem in its direct and outward expression that it is almost impossible to reconcile with its finality our persistent impression of tragic mystery in *Faustus*. How are we to reconcile the absence of tragic equilibrium in this, perhaps the most notable Satanic play in literature, with this recurrent and obstinate conviction that here, if anywhere, is tragedy? In part because the absence, even here, is more apparent than real. The framework of Marlowe's thought, the deductive process by which he arrives at his conclusion, is consistent and, within its limits, unassailable.[1] But there are indications that it did not take into account the whole of his experience. The Satanic reading of life may, it is true, permit Faustus (and Marlowe) to confound Hell in Elysium and see Helen's beauty fairer than the evening air; for if these are themselves destructible, by so much is the mockery of man's fate more hideous. But there is one thing that Marlowe cannot subjugate to that world-order that predestines universal damnation—his own inarticulate and hardly acknowledged conviction that it is evil. From what source springs this passionate judgement, he does not appear to consider; but ' Christ's blood streams in the firmament ' and there escapes —coherently, it may be, only in this single line—the implication of a deeper division in his mind, that his else consistent, Satanic interpretation has left unresolved. In that division, imaginatively revealed, though excluded from the logical demonstration of his thought, lie the dualism and conflict essential to the tragic mood. It does not constitute a balancing of one interpretation against another, but the

[1] It is remarkable, indeed, that so clear a piece of deduction should be conveyed (even though, of necessity, piecemeal) in strict dramatic form.

absolute Satanism is flawed and the reader left with the impression of a potential balancing force to challenge its absolutism. Thus, even in the extreme case of *Faustus*, the most nearly Satanic tragedy that can be found, it would appear that in so far as drama is Satanic it loses tragic balance and in so far as it is tragic it is not Satanic. Moreover, in Marlowe's play, though in less degree than in the tragedies of the centre, there is to be found the same balancing of content by form that we remarked in the work of Sophocles. A partial challenge to the suffering and evil in the outer action comes from that beauty of form and style which itself gives the lie to the implication that the fundamental order of things is evil. For this itself implies harmony; as in the work of Sophocles, though not so fully, the revelation of beauty in form is an unwitting testimony to that beneficence or immanent good of which beauty and form are manifestations.

Nevertheless, in the plays of this last group, absolute tragic balance is overset, although magnitude of passion and thought again become possible, since the action is related to a surrounding universe greater in scope and significance than the figures and events that make up that action. And even though the direct inference be to a universe of implacable evil, this does not detract from the grandeur, though it may from the wholeness and saneness of the final impression. Moreover, beyond this direct influence lies the indirect and seemingly unwitting testimony to the ' world of profit and delight ' that, residing in beauty, in form and in the unacknowledged sources of the poet's vision, maintains a partial balance in the play, despite his logical and intentional Satanism.

Admittedly, the suggestions we have just considered might, if pressed to the point of forming an argument, involve a *petitio principii*, inasmuch as the tragedies upon which we draw for evidence are themselves selected (even if unconsciously) by a mind in which the conclusion we later reach is already dormant. But they are suggestions only on the nature of certain perceived relations and Pascal's law still holds, for criticism as for much else : ' Tu ne me chercherais pas si tu ne m'avais connu.' The disability, in fact (if it be one), attaches to and must be acknowledged by all subjective criticism, and criticism is always in the last resort subjective. The logician himself admits that the conclusion of every syllogism is implicit in its major premiss and all that interpretation can do is to elucidate what is indeed obvious once it has been suggested.

The balance between the evil that is observed and the good that is guessed at is so common a part of human experience as to be perhaps its highest common factor. It is because tragedy reveals directly this equilibrium of conflicting thought and emotion that it has its enduring power. And it has been the attempt of this essay to indicate, first, that when tragedy departs from this norm and loses this correspondence with a universal experience it forfeits a part of its potency and, second, that this characteristic balance is the differentia of fine tragic art. In other words, it is precisely in this correspondence, and not in any of the outward characteristics by which the form can be described, that the essence of tragedy consists. It is then a mere matter of elucidation to indicate how and in what ways this balance is in practice preserved and by what deviations it may be destroyed. It may be observed in passing that the last three groups we considered, whether they were positive or negative, differed from the first, the religious drama, in that they destroyed the balance essential to the tragic mood by failing to satisfy that impression of two conflicting worlds of experience which reflects, at a certain phase, the totality of man's experience. Religious drama, on the other hand, supersedes the tragic mood by calling in the evidence of a wider surrounding universe of being, and destroys the balance by resolving the conflict.

It is now clear that tragedy is doubly subject to the law of limitation in art and that its subjection may throw some light upon the function of limitation itself. For it would appear to be subject not only to that which arises from its distinctive quality as an art, but to its own specific limitation in thought. The first of these conditions has been indicated in the preceding pages. The nature of the second, though implicit in what has there been said, may perhaps be briefly considered in conclusion.

Drama—and consequently tragedy, which can never escape the conditions common to all drama, but only refine upon and specialize them—must use as its primary material the world of experience, those events and actions which constitute actuality. It is its distinctive task to bring the presentation of these, by the resources of its peculiar technique, into the sharpest possible focus; to produce, that is, the impression of immediacy. The indications it can give of the interpenetrating world of spiritual reality must necessarily be reconciled to this (a task of rare difficulty) and are generally subordinated to it, though, as we have seen, the highest tragedy depends for its power and its authority on the presence of an element of this conflicting evidence in its total effect. When this underlying reality forces itself irresistibly upon the poet's mind, finding its way into positive expression, the balance of tragedy is likely to be overset. The play then, if it remain dramatic in any exact sense of the term, takes on a form which is in truth no longer that of tragedy; *Samson Agonistes* cannot strictly be called tragic, and Shakespeare passes through the phase of the great, balanced tragedies to a later form expressive of a change in the relative evaluation of the outer action and of the inner experience to which that action serves as manifestation. At this phase, common to the experience of many of the greatest dramatists, deed and event are, it would appear, primarily significant as images which make visible and manifest the reality which was hidden but immanent.[1] What we in part discern in Shakespeare's thought, as we pass from *Lear* to the three concluding plays of his career, has its parallel in the passage of Euripides from the middle plays to the *Bacchae*, of Sophocles from the first to the second *Oedipus*, of Ibsen from the social dramas to the group which culminates in *John Gabriel Borkman* and *When We Dead Awaken*.[2]

There are, moreover, certain writers who appear never to

[1] In great poetry they always have this function in some measure; they most certainly do so in Shakespeare's tragedies. But in the later phase to which I am referring, it becomes increasingly difficult to put any other simultaneous interpretation upon them.

[2] Goethe, less innately dramatic than any of these, could express his final interpretations in nothing less than the later additions to the second part of *Faust*.

touch the tragic mood. This mood is not, it need hardly be said, the prerogative of those who use the dramatic form called tragedy or denied to those whose age or race precludes it. Many writers in other forms, narrative verse or prose,[1] have revealed that perception of tragic balance which would in drama have produced tragedy; Virgil had, of all men, this note of the potential tragic poet; the world he saw was poised between those two conflicting interpretations that I have attempted to define; the influence of pain and evil at war with that of nobility in the spirit of man. But on the other hand many of the world's greatest poets have never touched this mood, and it must sometimes occur to the serious student of drama, and of its quintessence, tragedy, that their names are among the noblest and their thought among the most profound in poetry. Whereas Sophocles, Euripides, Shakespeare, Ibsen, even Aeschylus in the *Eumenides*, pass through and out of the tragic interpretation, Dante and Wordsworth never enter it in the fullness of their powers, and their major work is conceived in terms which do not allow of that Manichaeistic balance from which tragedy springs. And it is hard to resist the conclusion that the relation between their interpretation and that of tragedy as we have described it in these essays is, in fact, that of the double vision of the mystic to the vision focussed upon the manifestation only.[2]

And in essence this is what we suggested at the outset, that the religious interpretation of phenomena which means in fact the perception that they are only ' appearances ' is incompatible with tragedy, which forever doubts whether their significance is ultimate or relative. Religion, whether it be positive or Satanic, declares that the unseen world is real and the actual a varyingly transparent veil.[3] When, in its normal form, it is beatific, it transcends the tragic vision,

[1] We may instance, to go no further, Chaucer's *Troilus and Cresseide* and Tolstoy's *Anna Karenina*.

[2] As Mr. T. S. Eliot puts it (*Family Reunion*, Part II, Scene iii) :

> He sees the world as clearly as you or I see it,
> It is only that he has seen a great deal more than that.

[3] The materialistic interpretation, as we noticed earlier in this chapter, destroys the balance of tragedy equally effectively by seeing only the veil and declaring that ' there is no light behind the curtain '.

even as Fox's ocean of light and of love flowed over the ocean of darkness.   The ends of tragedy can never be served by that interpretation which, while seeing with it that ' in the world ye shall have tribulation ', sees also that which has ' overcome the world '.   For tragedy's concern is with that ' tribulation ' while it still fills man's consciousness to the exclusion of all but a doubtful and half-discerned promise of transvaluation.   In the next position, that of religious drama, the ' world ', which is the proper theatre of tragedy, has been ' overcome '; its seemingly solid structure has revealed itself as transparent in that irradiation which destroys the significance of outward event.

Tragedy then is an interim reading of life.   And in so far as it does not rest its interpretation upon that ultimate conclusion, in so far as it maintains that balance which is the source of its strength and of its value, to that extent it is the result of relative limitation of thought.   The paradox, again, is more apparent than real, for limitation, here also, has a specific function.   Just as, in the sphere of technique, we discovered that the limitation of the art afforded strength to the orthodox dramatists and transcendant power to those who successfully challenged it (whether in the major questions of theme and scope or in minor problems of presentation), so now we observe that it is on the relative limitation of its thought that its universal and enduring value depends. Precisely because it is an interim reading of life, it speaks to the condition of all but a few at some period of their lives ; for it reveals that balance, that uncertainty, which sees two worlds of being and cannot wholly accept either.   It speaks more potently to those within its reach than any other literary kind, because it reveals this interim reading in terms of those very technical limitations which impose upon it the necessity for concentration of form and directness of method.

APPENDIX

A note on the dramatic function of the prosody of *Samson Agonistes*.

THE prevailing movement of the opening passage, up to about the sixty-fifth line,[1] is slow, lifeless, and inert. The lines drag, like the thought. Sometimes they are deliberately unmusical and formless; they seem again and again about to drift into silence. When a feeble impulse revives the rhythmical movement and carries it forward again, it gives us no confidence that the impulse will last or the movement continue. This is the natural musical opening for the play; in these first phases Samson's mind, like his body, lies ' at random, carelessly diffus'd '.

> There am I wont to sit, when any chance
> Relieves me from my task of servile Toyl,
> Daily in the common Prison else enjoyn'd me,
> Where I a Prisoner chained, scarce freely draw
> The air imprison'd also, close and damp,
> Unwholsom draught : but here I feel amends,
> The breath of Heaven fresh-blowing, pure and sweet,
> With day-spring born; here leave me to respire.   (4–11.)

Passages of more vigour, in thought as in movement, break in here from time to time, but the inertia re-asserts its weight throughout the opening phases and even at intervals up to the entry of Dalila.

The next group of movements, from about l. 68 to about l. 187, has more range and flexibility. As Samson's mind tosses between dejection and sharp protest, the verbal music flashes from one extreme to the other of tempo and cadence, alternating between heavy, dragging verse and lines of the utmost irregularity, harsh in the pitch and relation of their sounds. The emotions are echoed with fidelity, even to the note of unassuageable grief in the iterated ' ai ' sounds of the long passage on blindness (ll. 68–109). There is more

---

[1] Line-divisions in the prosodic sequence are, except in a few cases where the end of a speech marks the end of a movement, a somewhat arbitrary way of indicating transitions. If I use them here I would prefer them to be regarded as approximations rather than precise divisions. The references in all cases are to the Oxford edition.

vigour, in sound as in feeling, than in the opening lines, but it is still undisciplined, restless, unsustained :

> The vilest here excel me,
> They creep, yet see, I dark in light expos'd
> To daily fraud, contempt, abuse and wrong,
> Within doors, or without, still as a fool,
> In power of others, never in my own;
> Scarce half I seem to live, dead more than half.
> O dark, dark, dark, amid the blaze of noon,
> Irrecoverably dark, total Eclipse
> Without all hope of day !   (73–82.)[1]

These characteristics are continued into the speeches of the chorus, but with modifications. The movement is less often sharp and restless, more often irresolute, wavering, uncertain. The verse, that is to say, is less stridently irregular, less full of contrasts in tempo and sound, but it more often lacks definition, drifting into broken fragments and cadences that are almost prose. It follows closely the emotions of the speakers, whose minds reveal by sympathy something of what is passing through Samson's. The choric verse at this point has a significant and organic relation to the verse of his speeches.[2]

In the passages that follow (ll. 187–448) there appear to be three related movements. First the short passages of dramatic verse which break in intermittently, as gusts of energy sweep over Samson's mind, disconnected still, but still gathering force. These passages have something of the immediacy of emotional speech in the hands of an experienced playwright; they unite with the cadences and tempo of dramatic verse those of familiar speech :

> And for a word, a tear,
> Fool, have divulged the secret gift of God
> To a deceitful Woman : tell me Friends,
> Am I not sung and proverb'd for a Fool
> In every street, do they not say, how well
> Are come upon him his deserts ?   Yet why ?   (200–5.)

---

[1] Cf. ll. 100–109 in the same speech, where the cadences of despondency recur with increased effect, after the vigorous protest and grief that have gone before.

[2] Cf. with the speech just examined, the movement of ll. 115–75, especially the transition from 115–27 to the middle of the speech and the similar transition, after l. 150, to the last part.

Second are the passages, steadily increasing in number, in which a steadier, firmer moulding of the verse begins to show, as the defensive mood of the debate and argument develops :

> That fault I take not on me, but transfer
> On *Israel's* Governours, and Heads of Tribes,
> Who seeing those great acts which God had done
> Singly by me against their Conquerours
> Acknowledged not, or not at all consider'd
> Deliverance offer'd.   (241–6.) [1]

Throughout this speech of Samson's there is a tendency (as here) for the lines to form into brief verse paragraphs, a rhythmic movement strictly in harmony with the growing cohesion of Samson's thought and passion.

In sharp contrast is the designed confusion, the wavering, weak rhythm of some of Manoa's speech (especially ll. 340–72). Perhaps the most important prosodic function of this passage is to emphasize the growing formal restraint and shapeliness of Samson's lines, especially of the speech (373–419) which immediately follows. Throughout this part the metres are all tending to greater smoothness and steadiness; even Manoa and the chorus are gradually affected by it.

In lines 448–709, which appear to constitute another prosodic group, we find for the first time (448–71) a complete verse paragraph, a musical passage which moves continuously from beginning to end and is composed of a sequence of related passages; a continuous passage of thought is now for the first time co-terminous with a speech. As the thought rises to a climax of conviction its mood is reflected in the prosodic movement; in the gradual quickening of pace and increase of emphasis and tension, in the momentary restlessness of lines 458–59 and in the sudden exhilaration as the movement becomes one of exultation (ll. 460–65). There is no need to analyse the strong, emphatic cadences of these lines, but we may note how far they are from the rhythms and sound-relations of the opening lines of the play. There is relaxation at the end of the passage, as the music and the emotion sink down again to quiescence.

[1] Cf. also ll. 373 *seq.*

The resignation that follows, though seeming at first glance a reversion to the dejection of the earlier part, is as clearly distinguished from it prosodically as it is psychologically. This is a slow and even movement—lacking variation, it is true, and strong emphases, but musical and not formless :

> All otherwise to me my thoughts portend,
> That these dark orbs no more shall treat with light,
> Nor th' other light of life continue long,
> But yield to double darkness nigh at hand :
> So much I feel my genial spirits droop,
> My hopes all flat, nature within me seems
> In all her functions weary of herself.   (590–96.)

This is followed by a series of passages (606–709) in which Samson's doubts beset him again, and the prosody, following the inner turmoil, returns to a restless movement, fiercer than the corresponding earlier passages,[1] just as the steadier movements now are firmer. Coherence and definition of thought or emotion are followed closely by the corresponding prosodic distinction.

In the next passage (the arrival of Dalila and the rising dispute between her and Samson), the prosody, like the thought, shows a steady increase of firmness and form. The verse becomes tough and resilient; it hardens as the moods and tempers harden.

> Such pardon therefore as I give my folly,
> Take to thy wicked deed : which when thou seest
> Impartial, self-severe, inexorable,
> Thou wilt renounce thy seeking, and much rather
> Confess it feigned, weakness is thy excuse,
> And I believe it, weakness to resist
> Philistian gold.   (825–31.) [2]

This steady metallic rhythm is the fitting accompaniment to the hard mood of dispute and debate,[3] and gives stability

---

[1] See particularly ll. 617–27.

[2] Compare also the whole passage, 748–959.

[3] There is no room here for a detailed analysis of the technique, but we may perhaps notice three things which contribute to this effect. The contrast between light and strong stresses in the individual feet is reduced, both strong and light approximating, in many cases, to half accents, a stress midway between both; by this means the spring of the lines is subdued; the method is precisely the opposite of that by which Marlowe, for example, emphasizes the throb of the individual line in the

to the prosodic foundation from now onward. When the
exultant movement already noticed in an earlier phase
returns,[1] it grows out of this tougher verse and becomes
itself firmer and more even, passing into a grave, majestic
movement which increasingly reflects the growing assurance
and clarity of Samson's spirit :

> Be of good courage, I begin to feel
> Some rousing motions in me which dispose
> To something extraordinary my thoughts.
> I with this messenger will go along,
> Nothing to do, be sure, that may dishonour
> Our Law, or stain my vow of *Nazarite.*
> If there be aught of presage in the mind,
> This day will be remarkable in my life
> By some great act, or of my days the last.   (1381–89.)[2]

After an interval on a lower level, reflecting the false
relief of Manoa and the chorus, there is a passage of rising
excitement gathered together by the messenger's speech.
This part (1426–end) shows a gradual lowering of tension
from the sublimity of Samson's final mood towards the con-
versational tempo of verse in the drama of everyday life;
from this it is guided again through the messenger's speech
into the final movement, in which extreme simplicity, of
blank verse and choric ode alike, mirrors the serenity of the
end of the play. The rhythm is now strongly marked and
regular, but the variations are reduced again and we reach a
prosody which in its compactness and stability is in complete
contrast with the opening phases of the play.[3]

---

main passages of *Tamburlaine*. In the second place, the lines are
relatively regular, with little substitution or inversion (accentual
anaepaest, spondee, pyrrhic, or trochee) and the comparatively level
feet are allowed to succeed each other with little variation from the
prosodic base. In the third place, the tempo does not vary greatly
from line to line (rapidly spoken lines of multisyllabic words are not
followed by and contrasted with the slow paces of lagging mono-
syllables), so that there is little elasticity in the lines groups. Thus
each prosodic unit from the smallest (the individual foot) through the
single line to the larger unit of the line-group plays its part in producing
this complex sound effect that so accurately reflects the state of mind
of the speaker.

[1] See ll. 1076–1426 and compare the earlier passage, ll. 460–65.
[2] Cf. also 1423–26.
[3] See especially 1711–14, 1745–48.

INDEX

[This is only a brief list of references and is not intended to be exhaustive. Those topics and names only that occur most often in the text are listed here.]

153

PRINTED IN GREAT BRITAIN BY RICHARD CLAY AND COMPANY LTD.,
BUNGAY, SUFFOLK.